BODY SHAPERS
DREAM TEAM

BODY SHAPERS DREAM TEAM

UNUSUAL PEOPLE, UNUSUAL EXPERIMENT

David Singer

Body Shapers Dream Team © 2018 David Singer

www.davidsingerauthor.com

This book is a work of fiction.
However, the dieting suggestions contained in the story are bona fide.

This book is not intended as a substitute for professional medical advice. The reader should consult a physician in health matters, particularly with respect to any symptoms that may require diagnosis and medical attention.

Cover design: Tony Grida

Editor: Darby O'Shaughnessy

ISBN: 978-1-9876982-0-6 (print)
Library of Congress Control Number: 2018904735

Printed in the United States of America

DEDICATION

To everyone who struggles to gain weight;
to everyone who struggles to lose weight;
to those who try to remain as they are;
to those who have had difficulty finding the right person
because of their weight; and
to those unusual people who go out of their way
to make a difference in the lives of others.

TABLE OF CONTENTS

PROLOGUE

My name is Mitch. My weight is normal, and I regard over-weight people as disorganized, overstressed, or depressed—people who think that by eating, they will feel better and their problems will diminish or disappear. These wishful thinking men and women do not see the reality of life. They do not see how their future appearance, health, and job-searches will be affected. They do not see the harassing and bullying that their obesity will generate. Eating seems to make them happy and jolly. In fact, some people believe that in addition to being kinder and friendlier, fat people are more considerate, sensitive, and astute.

I had just finished my studies at Hofstra University in Hempstead, Long Island. My family had done their best to help me, but they had other kids to put through college. My father told me in an apologetic voice, "Mitch, we love you, but you're on your own now." Those words echoed in my mind every morning when I got up, and I realized that I really was on my own.

I cashed my last scholarship check and used the money to move closer to my temporary summer job as a reporter for a fledgling newspaper in metropolitan New York—a job for which young graduates from all over the country had applied. Thus, whatever I did has to be outstanding because too many people were after my job, and I was hoping this job would become permanent.

Everyone wants to work in New York. As the saying goes, "If you can make it in New York, you can make it anywhere." Since a thousand more reporters were trying to land the permanent position, my only chance of making this job last was to impress the boss. So I decided to do a study on what overweight people think—for example, what overweight people actually think when criticized. My secondary objective was to gather enough information to create a weight gain/weight loss program that would be accepted as *modus operandi* for people who needed to gain weight—and especially for those who wanted to lose weight fast.

I devised a plan . . .

THE PLAN

My plan is simple. For one month, I will gain weight as fast as possible. The following month, I will lose the weight I gained and return to my normal weight of 154 pounds. Then I will meet people with extreme weight problems to identify the causes and why they remain as they are. With all this information, I will devise the preeminent weight gain/weight loss program of all time. Meanwhile, to continue living in New York, I need to find a roommate to share the rent.

I've started to research how to gain weight as fast as possible. To keep an accurate record of what I eat, I'm adding daily frequency and weight to my month's chart.

Following this month of extreme overeating, I will lose the weight I gained. The idea is to gain weight, and then reduce as fast as possible until I get back to my original weight.

My first objective is to meet two people, one very fat and one very thin. I need their inputs into what makes them remain the way they are. I have to figure out how to go about meeting these people. I could always go to Overeaters Anonymous (OA), an organization that caters to compulsive eaters. Plenty of people attend those meetings. I've read that OA has over 100 meetings a week in NYC, Brooklyn, and Queens. They advertise that, unlike other organizations, OA offers a program of recovery—of weight loss or, for very thin people, weight gain. OA also addresses the emotional and physical well-being of their members. OA seems like a good place to start. But first, I need a roommate. The rent for a one bedroom apartment is too expensive, so I decide to try my luck on Craigslist.

In personals I advertise my disposition and my willing-ness to negotiate the sleeping arrangements and to share all kitchen and cleaning responsibilities. Of course, I have to im-pose conditions. I need someone who isn't a slob, who has normal drinking habits, and who absolutely is a non-smoker without a drug habit. Not wanting to be bothered with phone calls, I post a new email I created specifically for this purpose.

I will start my project next Monday with a visit to *The Daily Flash* on 14th Street. I am not required to stay in the office, but I am expected to report every morning and sign in, say hello to my department boss, Mr. Perry Petro, and leave—unless I need to use the office computer, of course. I tried to be friendly with some of the office personnel on my initial interview, but they ignored me. I guess they had be-come accustomed to the constant flow of young summer-job applicants. *Just one of the bunch will be accepted only to leave after a ten-week stint, never to be seen again, so why bother building an office camaraderie*—or so I imagined.

In hindsight, I'm surprised that I was chosen. I wonder what quality Mr. Petro detected in me that he liked. Was it my intense blue eyes? Was it my curriculum? Was it my abilities as a Hofstra champion ping pong player? I don't know for sure. Probably his wife, of whom he seems very fond, influenced his choice since she also attended Hofstra University. His office is filled with pictures of her.

I look everywhere and find that renting an apartment for only ten weeks is not easy— especially a furnished apartment close to a bus or subway stop. Then I get lucky; Craigslist works for me. A student emails saying she needs her apartment occupied for ten weeks. She has gotten a summer job in Memphis and wants to sub-let to me. I'm thrilled to land such an exact arrangement.

Carol is a fastidious person. She begs me to return the apartment in as excellent a condition as she is giving it to me. Well, I will definitely try.

When I met her at a nearby Starbucks, she was twisting a strand of hair and gnawing on a fingernail. She confided that she was afraid about meeting someone through Craigslist after all the stories that had been written about bad experiences. But the moment she met me and looked into my incredible blue eyes, her facial expression changed. She smiled or blushed, and she actually invited me for a coffee and shared a sandwich she had brought with her. Later, when she took me up to show me her apartment, I thought she would

3

jump me, but I was wrong. I guess that my imagination does not comply totally with reality.

I've had my share of adventures, especially while in school. Mostly they were one-night stands with girls I picked up at the local beer joints, and, since not one of them created real interest by possessing the qualities I wanted, I'd slipped away after a fast and uncomplicated moment.

It occurs to me that Carol, my new landlady, does have some of the qualities I look for in a woman. She's pretty, she has class, she's careful, and she's neat. She's also educated and intelligent. Of course, that's my first impression. I should also mention that she's thin.

I have never been with an overweight woman. Maybe that's because none have been around during my beer drinking moments, or maybe none thought they had a chance with a guy like me. Who knows? Beer joints are not the only places I meet women. I grew up in a town where many women were available, so probably my interest in sports beat out my interest in looking for girls. Or maybe I didn't want girls to know where I lived and how to find me in case something uncomfortable happened between us.

No time for pondering the past now. I have my plan and my apartment. I need to get on with my project. I need to meet a very fat person and a very thin person.

CHAPTER 2

I MEET MISS SHIRLEY

On Sunday, I decide to explore what is within walking distance of my rental. I'm surprised to find everything a person might need: bakeries, health spas, gyms, and incredible restaurants that I can't afford—all right here. Next, I discover plenty of small bars and fast food joints that will satisfy my daily needs.

During my neighborhood exploration I stumble upon Zabar's, home of the world's most incredible cheeses, lox, breads, chocolates, and a million other products. They really do have every delicacy you can think of. Of course Zabar's is off-limits to my pocket, but at least I know where it is.

Today I discover *Dive 75*, a bar that's not actually a dive. They have board games in case I get bored. They also have a colossal tropical fish tank, which is probably why I think that *Dive 75* is going to be my main hangout. The fish are beautiful. Since I was a kid, I always dreamed of having my own fish tank, but—here comes the excuse again: Fish cost money, and a fish tank with fish requires maintenance, feed-ing, cleaning. That's why I don't have one. Sometimes I feel like a gypsy because I move frequently, often out of bore-dom. I tire easily and look for new environments. How can I even think of an aquarium?

I approach the bar and sit next to an obese young woman seated on a bar stool. I search for her feet; they're hanging by the stool. She's fat *and* small.

"Hi," I say with a smile, nodding in her direction. She is preoccupied with sipping something that I cannot identify. After I start my first beer, I try again. "Could you please pass the peanuts?" *Or what little is left of them.*

With disdain, she places the peanut dish by my beer.

"Thanks. I'm Mitch. I just moved to this neighborhood." She barely nods and continues sipping.

I am determined to make her talk. I begin humming the newest song on the world charts, and that makes her look at me—with a smile. Apparently I hit upon a favorite of hers.

"I'm Shirley—from Montana," she adds. She tells me that she is a student at Julliard in Lincoln Center, which makes me think that she must be brilliant. Julliard is the place to be accepted if you have unusual musical talent. I look her straight in the eye, trying to get her to notice my eyes. When she finally does, her eyes light up—

Bum ba bum bumbum ba bahhh bum. She digs her cell phone from her bag and has a heated conversation with someone about not being able to go to a concert alone. When she finally hangs up, anger shows in her face.

"What happened?" I ask.

Without taking her eyes from mine, she says, "My friend just told me that there's a concert in two hours in New Jersey, but it's so far from here. I'm a long way from Montana, and I don't know how to get around New York City yet."

My mind has already computed that Shirley is an ideal fat person for my plan. All I have to do is win her over. "One thing I'm expert at," I say with my best smile, "is how to get around the Tri-State Area. If you'd like, I'd be happy to accompany you to the concert."

"You would? Oh, thank you so much!"

I finish my beer, and we hurry out of the bar. At her five feet, two inches and my five feet, eleven inches, we make a strange-looking couple running to catch a bus to Port Authority. Once onboard I glance at Shirley. She has a distinctly beautiful face: very narrow, with full lips, a slightly larger-than-average distance between her eyes, high cheek bones, narrow eyebrows, and no eye circles. *If she were taller and less fat, she'd be my type of girl.* Anyway, I believe that Shirley is the beginning of my story: She is beautiful, intelligent—and very fat. A thought runs through my mind. Should I attempt to seduce her? The way she walks is sexy, and she has a sensual grin—but no. I don't think she's that type. Who knows? But I'm not going to try.

THE CONCERT

We arrive on time. Fortunately, because the concert is free, we don't need to spend extra money. I'm hungry, so I buy two gigantic kosher hot dogs. Shirley thoroughly enjoys hers.

This hot dog may have opened up her heart to me because, as we finish eating, she grabs my hand and leans on me. She becomes extremely friendly. I think I have just found my gateway to her inner feelings: food.

Shirley meets her friend, an older woman with whom her family has connections. The lady is supposed to be Shirley's advisor in Manhattan. She is unhappy to see that Shirley has company, and she sits far from us.

The band, a new group from Helsinki, is doing a USA tour. I find their music far from impressive, but Shirley enjoys it, so I hang in until the end.

On the ride back to our neighborhood, we exchange phone numbers. Shirley would like to continue our adventure—or so it seems—but I have too many things on my mind at that moment. I explain that I am beginning a new job and have to get up early. She understands and asks if she can call me. I continue in an extra friendly mode, telling her how happy I am to have met such a special artist—she loves that line. And she hugs me again. I give her an intense hug and leave her at her studio apartment—which is not far from my flat.

CHAPTER 4

THE OFFICE

I get up earlier than usual. For my graduation, I received an Amazon Echo, the incredible WiFi connected, hands-free speaker you control with your voice. I told Alexa to wake me with Harry Belafonte's music—and she did!

I arrive at my new office on time. I check in and visit Mr. Petros. He smiles. "I suggest that you begin your project immediately." He hints that if I do something really special, I will be rewarded with glory and satisfaction. I laugh at the comment and consider it advice.

I have my eye on one special secretary in the office—not because she's anything special to look at, but because I have a feeling that she is in command here, and especially in command of the department to which I report. She has a Latin name, Esperanza. I approach her with care.

"Hi, I'm Mitch." Esperanza is preoccupied on the computer. "I'm going to get a *cortadito*, and I wondered if you'd like one."

She stops and looks up—and into my big, deep, ocean-blue eyes, waiting for her to explore.

She stares intently, falling into my trap. «¿Hola, cómo estás?»

I know enough Spanish to respond, «Mejor que nunca» (better than ever).

She smiles. "You have a way with busy women. I like that."

«¿ Con Splenda o azucar?»

"Gracias. Con Sweet 'N Low."

And that's it. She will be my ally for the duration; I'm sure of that. Esperanza tells me she has a niece who would probably love to go out with an Americano with such beautiful eyes.

"I would love to meet a beautiful Latin girl," I tell her. I also explain that I have very little money to take her to nice places.

Esperanza laughs at the connotation. "Good luck with your project," she says. "My capacity is limited, but let me know if I can help you in any way."

Soon after we drink our *cortaditos,* I leave. I have work to do.

OVEREATERS ANONYMOUS

I begin searching for Overeaters Anonymous—the program's objectives, methods, philosophy. What I notice first are their advertising come-ons: "YOU ARE NOT ALONE ANYMORE"; "No matter what your food problems are—*compulsive overeating, undereating, food addiction, anorexia, bulimia, binge eating, or over-exercising*—we have a solution." Their message was clear.

OA is a group of anonymous individuals who share experiences, strengths, and hopes in order to combat their weight problems. They charge no dues and are self-supporting through contributions. They have no religious or political affiliations. They use a twelve-step pathway to recovery. OA claims that their system works, and that most members are able to go forward and lead productive lives. OA members number over sixty thousand in more than 6,500 different groups that meet in over seventy-five countries. Their headquarters are in New Mexico.

OA defines *compulsion* as "any impulse or feeling of being irresistibly driven toward the performance of some irrational act." They go on to define *compulsive overeating* as a "progressive and addictive illness" that they view as a "chronic condition and an attempt to alleviate psychological stress."

OA provides newcomers with a questionnaire containing questions like *Do you give too much time and thought to food?* If newcomers answer yes to three such questions, OA accepts them because these responses indicate that a problem exists with which the organization feels it can be of assistance.

I need more information on abstinence, which is how Alcoholics Anonymous (AA) trains its members. AA advocates that members abstain from drinking alcohol. Some counter by pointing out that alcoholics do not have to drink, but compulsive eaters still have to eat.

OA responds that the AA people do have to drink—just not alcohol—and that overeaters have to eat, but not the foods that trigger their compulsive eating. The OA program suggests that members identify the foods that trigger overeating.

I can't believe my good luck. OA sounds ideal for my project. OA members are fat, so they'll be able to tell me what made them gain weight and why they didn't lose it. Since they're at OA, they want to stop overeating—which means they will lose weight, and this reducing dovetails perfectly with my weight loss program. Surely one OA member will agree to participate in my project. Now all I have to do is find a thin volunteer.

CHAPTER 6

SEARCH FOR A THIN VOLUNTEER

My objectives are becoming clear. I need to convince a person like Shirley to lose weight by all the means already known—following 100% health-safety measures, of course. Then I need to enlist a thin person who will gain weight doing exactly the opposite of what OA suggests for a period of one month. I will do both: I will overeat with abandon for one month, and then I will try to lose those excess pounds. I will use three different measures: First, what to do for fat people who want to lose weight; second, what to do for thin people who want to gain weight; and third, what to do for normal people like me who go on temporary overeating binges or binge diets.

I set out for a vegan restaurant on Broome Street to find out what vegans eat. The restaurant is packed. I decide to try a smoked teriyaki *seitan*, which is inexpensive and turns out to be very tasty. Looking over the crowd, I spot a young man searching for a place to sit down. He's so thin that I wonder how he is able to stand on his feet. I gesture indicating that there is room next to me. He's delighted to find a friendly New Yorker, and immediately he moves to where I'm sitting.

Kim is an American-born Vietnamese, around twenty-six years old and full of smiles. He's very friendly indeed. I tell him about my summer job, and he tells me that he works in a nearby printing company. He is well-educated and in charge of the company's technical side.

I tell him about my project, and to my surprise, he offers to help. "How do you think you can help?" I ask.

"Well," Kim says, "as you can see, I'm significantly underweight. People make me feel like a strange rarity, the way they look at me as if I'm a sicko. I'm not. In fact, I'm not even vegan. My metabolism is strange. I eat normal, healthy quantities and never gain a pound."

"Do you exercise?"

"I guess I do exercise a lot. At the gym, they call me a 'hard gainer' or 'ectomorph.' I don't know if being an ectomorph is genetic or not. I just know there's a lot of misinformation on the subject."

"Kim, you're a perfect fit for my plan. In fact, you're such an incredible find that if you'd like, you can be a partial partner."

"What do you mean, a partial partner?"

I tell him that I plan to write a book on my findings. "If things go well with my book, I will give you a portion of the benefits." We exchange information and make a dinner date for the next day.

I am so happy. In such a short time, I have a clear idea, and—if Shirley agrees—two subjects for my experiment.

CHAPTER 7

SHIRLEY'S THOUGHTS

I am twenty-one years old. All my life, I've been an anxious overeater. My whole family are overeaters, and each generation seems to copy these overeating habits. I can't do much about it. I've tried, believe me, but food soothes my emotional pain—while at the same time making me fatter.

Over the years, as I've continued to gain weight, I've hated myself even more. I don't believe anyone thinks fat is sexy. I never wanted to admit that I'm a sugar junkie unable to control what she puts into her mouth, but when I look in the mirror and compare myself with normal-looking girls, I see reality. I see that sooner or later, I will need to take my problem seriously and combat it.

I was the top student in high school, and I just finished college *summa cum laude*. Music is my only hobby. I learned to play piano, sax, harp, guitar, and just about all the rest of the musical instruments. That's why I've been accepted with a full scholarship to Julliard for a post-graduate degree.

I have great difficulty making friends. They end up making fun of me or bullying me, so I eat alone. I'm a loner in general, and people seem to respect that. Yesterday, when I met Mitch, I couldn't believe that he was actually pleasant and friendly—and he's a hunk of a man. Why did he sit next to me, and why did he start talking to me? No one has ever done that before. Mitch said he would call me. I doubt it, but he said I could call him, and maybe he will . . . No, I don't think so. Meeting him was too good to be true. His eyes—wow! What a man! I've never had a boyfriend. I've never gone to anything with anyone until Mitch went to the concert with me—and he held my hand. I hugged him, and he hugged me back! Good things are happening to me in New York.

I need to discuss the time when I was in college and another fat student introduced me to a cousin of hers over the phone. We began chatting. I didn't expect us to develop real feelings on the phone, but when we started talking, appearances weren't an issue. As time went by, we unexpectedly hit it off, and feelings began to develop. When he hinted that he'd like to meet in person, I was the one who complicated our chatting relationship. That he lived in Texas and I was in Montana was a further complication. The idea of letting him know that I was as fat as his cousin horrified me. Oh, he saw pictures of my face on the Internet, but never my body. I am short with big boobs, and few men enjoy looking at my body. My insecurity and the prospect of immense disappointment made the relationship disappear.

I was going to join one of the organizations that helps direct members' eating habits, like FA—Food Addicts, or OA—Overeaters Anonymous, but everyone seems to have a different opinion as to how successful each one is, so I always put it off.

CHAPTER 8

DAY TWO

Alexa awakens me with the weather forecast: *Today is going to be hot.* Summers in New York City can be hectic, hot, and stressful—especially when the subway air conditioning fails. I reach the office on time, check in, and head straight to my new ally Esperanza—with a fresh *cortadito.*

"I'm going to get used to these," she warns, closing her eyes and inhaling the coffee's aroma. "I must make sure that this summer job of yours becomes permanent."

I smile my most winning smile. "If you do that, I'll meet your niece."

Esperanza smiles back. "Do a selfie with me, so I can show Graciela." We take the selfie.

"Esperanza, out of curiosity, do you happen to have a recent picture of Graciela?"

"I thought you'd never ask." Esperanza whips out her phone. She scrolls through the photos until she finds the one she wants and turns the phone toward me.

Wow! Graciela is something else. I didn't know such incredible beauties existed.

Noticing my staring, Esperanza says, "Well, she *is* Venezuelan," and adds, "where many of the Miss Universe winners are produced."

"Okay, Esperanza. As soon as I receive my first check, I'll invite her for coffee. I'm a poor gringo, you know." We both laugh.

I decide to visit my friend Scott who has started a medical residency at NYU Medical Center. I call, and he says he can have lunch with me at the clinic. He is a warm and smart friend, and sure to be an excellent physician one day. We arrange to meet in the hospital's cafeteria.

The cafeteria is full of people coming and going, all in a tumultuous rush to eat and return to work. Scott is on time. He brings along a man—a fifty-year-old, grossly-obese man—whom he introduces as Uncle Marvin.

"Uncle Marvin just dropped by, and he hasn't had lunch. I hope you don't mind."

"No, of course not. No problem, Scott." Before Scott can decide what to pick up at the food carousel, his beeper goes off.

He jumps and says apologetically, "Emergency. Please excuse me." He dashes off and leaves me with Uncle Marvin.

Uncle Marvin is a talker. "I've made it forty-eight years without a heart attack or a stroke—or any disease, for that matter. I know that I'm obese, so I'm a living time bomb. I've lost weight many times, but I gain it back. Diet books are full of baloney. I've counted calories, exercised abnormally. I eat fat free, sugar free, and I've gone through starvation diets—all to no avail. Then I read a book by an endocrinologist who talks about controlling the insulin and not the calories—in other words, a low-carb diet. This doc also believes that exercising isn't effective in weight loss.

"Granted, in my case, arrogance has a lot to do with my overweight. At one time, I was so fat that I had difficulty going to the bathroom. I could not use urinals in public bathrooms because I could not hold my pants and grab myself. When I needed to wipe, I could not reach my wiping area. I had to do maneuvers and twist in many directions until I could wipe myself. I avoided going to bathrooms outside my apartment. Only at home could I find comfort.

"Now that I've lost a few pounds, I can reach myself easier. I still need help to take a shower since I can't reach every part of my body. I have difficulty inserting a belt through the loops with my pants on. Putting on socks is a thirty-minute ordeal. I use shoes without laces, and sometimes, wearing slippers has been my only solution. Everything is a problem. Sex? Forget it. I've forgotten it. Buying new clothes is difficult, and sometimes even impossible to attempt. New styles do not exist for me. My poor wife has had to deal with food shopping and carrying groceries for ten people while in reality, everything was for me."

We finish our tuna fish sandwiches. When Uncle Marvin sees that I am not eating my chips, he asks for them. When he finishes, he wants to buy some more—only getting up to do so is difficult for him. I tell him that I have to run, but first ask if he would be willing to help me with my experiment. After a quick explanation of my work, he agrees, and we exchange phone information.

At that moment, Scott calls. He says that he has a complicated case and will call me that night. I understand.

CENTRAL PARK

En route to Central Park, I quickly jot down invaluable information that Uncle Marvin has inadvertently supplied. I have never been to the park, but I have to experiment. I notice the fabulous views; a small zoo with monkeys; a big carousel, and a conservatory garden. In Sheep Meadow, I stop to rest. Strange people abound, making people-watching one hell of an experience.

A young child bumps into me and falls down. I am about to reach down to help him when a lady runs over and picks him up. A gracious woman, she thanks me—and then starts crying. "Tommy, how many times have I told you that you must be more careful?"

"Don't worry," I interject. "No damage has been done."

She thanks me again, but I'm not listening. I'm staring at the child who is unusually thin.

"I know what you're thinking," she says accusingly. "My son is too skinny." She shakes her head. "Don't think that being skinny means a person is healthy, mister. Tommy has MONW—Metabolically Obese Normal Weight. People with MONW are under-lean but over-fat. Some people call it 'skinny fat.' In other words, it's better to be fat-normal than skinny-out-of-shape. I'm afraid my son will soon develop diabetes. He'll be at twice the risk for death than if he was fat and developed diabetes. Perhaps having the extra pounds keeps a person safer."

MONW is all new to me, and I know I need to learn much more. It occurs to me that having young people in my experiment would be an added positive. Studies on teenagers, for example, have found that 37% of skinny children have one or more signs of pre-diabetes caused by high blood pressure, high blood sugar, and high cholesterol. One third of children in the USA are overweight or obese. These statistics are factors in my research, so I will need a teenager who is skinny and one who is obese. But how will I find them? And how will I convince them to volunteer for my study?

CHAPTER 10

SHIRLEY ALMOST BECOMES A VOLUNTEER

t's still early when I arrive home, so I call Shirley. She is at school practicing piano. She is overwhelmed by my call, and without hesitation agrees to meet. I tell her that I will be right over and that I want to hear her music. I jog across the park to the West Side and onto Broadway and Lincoln Center Plaza.

The Julliard School is a performing arts conservatory and the best known music school in the USA. Julliard's acceptance rate is lower than that of any university I know—less than 7.6 % of all applicants. So the students they admit have to be really good.

Shirley sent me her location through WhatsApp, so I easily find her playing a large Bösendorfer, an Austrian piano. I don't recognize what she is playing, but it sounds wonderful. If her intention is to show off, she is successful.

We chat for a while, and then I ask if she wants to have an early dinner-picnic in Central Park. Wow, she loves the idea, so we proceed further up the West Side to find a farmers market she mentions having seen that closes at 7 p.m. We walk the few blocks to the market, and I stop to admire a bin of ripe red tomatoes.

"Let's buy healthy ingredients," I suggest. She agrees, of course. Being with me and going on a picnic together is a fantasy come true for her. We buy a ready-mixed salad with low-fat Italian dressing, and decide to share a sardine wrap with some hummus spread. We also buy some water. She insists they we share the cost, to which I readily agree, since I've been honest with her about my economic situation, which she accepts without hesitation.

Shirley's morning had been melancholic, but that has totally changed. She is experiencing the effects of a super-production of high-esteem hormone. I am so much the gentleman, respecting every word she says, looking at her with sincere admiration—all of which are totally new to her. Our dinner-picnic is, in fact, her first date ever—or is it a date? I imagine what she's thinking:

> *Well, what does it matter if it's a date or not? He's with me, and he could easily be with a million beautiful normal-weight woman in this city. He really is handsome. I'm going to have to do something fast. I need to lose weight immediately. No more chips, chocolate, hot fudge*

sundaes. No more junk food. I need to consult someone if I'm going to change. I may have found what I've been waiting for—a chance to be normal.

I'm having a really good time myself, I realize. Shirley's smart—*really* smart—and she's ideal for my experiment. She has a beautiful face. Okay, she's short, but she has a sexy voice and she knows how to talk to a man. And she's a doer, I have no doubt. She's going to be successful in whatever she does in the future. She is one cool broad. I'm going to convince her to lose her excess weight and keep it off.

After our picnic, we walk down the lanes of Central Park, sometimes holding hands, sometimes telling ourselves stories that don't have an end.

That evening, I realize that things are getting dangerously intimate. I cannot let our feelings interfere with my summer project. I kiss her lightly and call it a night. I do not enlist her for the experiment—yet.

DAY THREE

Alexa is perfect because the Wi-Fi in this building is fast and reliable, the best I have used. She wakes me with a joke—not a good joke, but it makes me laugh. Things are going well. At the Daily Flash, Mr. Petro asks how I'm doing.

"All is in order. I'm organizing an incredible experiment."

"Very good," he says, nodding. "I won't ask what you're planning because that's your business."

I see that he's in a good mood, and this gives me the courage to ask, "Will there be any extra pocket money for my expenditures?" He does not answer. I understand and proceed to Esperanzas' desk with the prepared *cortadito*. She greets me with a smile.

"Graciela was impressed that I chose such a handsome man for her. But you'll have to wait to meet her because she's a waitress on a cruise ship that left today for Europe."

"That's okay. By the time she returns, I'll have some money to take her out."

Esperanza grins.

"Is there any way to persuade Mr. Petro to give me pocket money for my expenses while I'm on assignment for the newspaper?"

"I'll see what I can do," she says. "I'll let you know soon."

I leave and call Dr. Scott again. He says he can meet me at 5 p.m. at Bruno's coffee shop. He only has forty-five minutes because he plans to take a train to Long Island for a meeting. That's okay with me because at 6:30 I have an appointment to meet Kim.

I head to a fast weight-loss center in Midtown to see what they offer and find a very friendly receptionist. (I say very friendly because my experience has been the opposite; New York is different.) I explain that I have come to the center searching for a place to send my sister who has to lose forty pounds.

"Oh, I knew you weren't here for you, because you look great," she says with a smile. "Don't *you* go on a diet."

I return the smile and look straight into her eyes. The effect is magical. She blushes and blurts, "You have the most beautiful blue eyes I've ever seen."

"Do you want to meet for coffee?" I ask, hoping to capitalize on the moment.

She moves out from behind her desk to afford me full view of her curvaceous body. I nod appreciatively. "My, oh my! You have one helluva body!" She gives me a slow, sexy demonstration with a very sexy walk, grinning, insinuating, then sashays back to her desk and hands me a flyer listing the company's services.

"We also offer customized plans, see?" She points to the top of the brochure. "Our system is the HCG Diet." *Phentermine script and lipotropic injections for patients who qualify.*

"What criteria do you follow?"

She tells me that it depends on the lab work and the patient's medical history.

"Phentermine is an appetite suppressant, isn't it?"

"Yes, it's a sympathomimetic amine, a stimulant similar to an amphetamine. With controlled exercise, phentermine works. Of course," she adds, "not all patients can take phentermine. We have to be careful with high blood pressure patients and those with related problems."

"How about the lipotropic injections?"

"They help breakdown and metabolize fat."

"Are they safe?"

She looks at me narrowly. "The doctors at this clinic are very careful to whom they administer these injections—and so we haven't had problems."

"Like what kind of problems?" I persist.

"We've been *told* that following the injections, side effects may include infections, inflammation, disfigurement, and even death. However, we're aware of these possible reactions, so we're extremely careful."

I nod. "Do you use vitamin B-12 injections?"

She shakes her head. "I don't think so. Their effectivity has not been proven, so we wouldn't use them."

"I'm aware that other diet institutes believe in them."

She shrugs.

"I congratulate you," I say. "You're remarkably knowledgeable for a receptionist."

She looks pleased. "I'm almost finished with my postgraduate degree in psychology. I study at night because I need to work."

I tell her about my project. She listens, nodding. When I finish, she hands me a business card from the holder on her desk. "In case you need psychological advice with your experiment," she says with a smile. "Now, tell me the truth. You don't have an overweight sister, do you? You came in for information for your experiment."

I smile back, giving her the full benefit of my pearly whites, and she reads the truth in my expression.

"I promise to take you up on that coffee." After we exchange telephone numbers, she adds, "If you want to talk with someone who admires your eyes, call me. I'm Kathy."

I still have a few hours to kill, so I wander around before heading back to Central Park where I stop at a hot dog vendor's for a potato knish brunch. In recent days I have not been having my regular breakfasts. In fact, I have not been doing any of my usual exercises, or the daily twenty-five laps that I used to swim in Hofstra's pool. I'm getting out of shape.

At the park, I stop by the small zoo to observe the monkeys' behavior. *Why do animals in the wild never become fat?* The only fat animals are pigs and chickens who are overfed by humans so they'll produce more meat. It appears that most animals do not suffer from human problems. So animals don't have stress—or do they? The survival of many species depends on their finding enough food and water, a problem in some areas of the world. Of course, there's always the possibility of an animal becoming another animal's meal, which must be a constant daily stress for them. If so, then my theory that animals do not experience stress is wrong.

That overweight is a factor in the causes of anxiety is well-known. Some say *I was getting anxious,* attributing their overeating to anxiety. They maintain that the anxious person eats more to diminish feelings of anxiety. Others say that in some cases, anxiety causes people to *lose* weight. These theories remain unresolved. A tipping point must exist where, in response to feelings of anxiety, a person either overeats or avoids food. A logical thought pattern says that if we find the exact tipping point between the two extremes, we can avoid becoming fat or skinny.

Inactivity is another mistake for those who are stressed. Exercise reduces muscle tension and releases neurotransmitters that boost people's moods and at the same time burn stress hormones.

I strolled to the lake area and noticed a bunch of youngsters with two camp counselors. The counselor nearest me was having a tough time stopping the youngsters from hurling stones at the ducks in the water. I approached him and said, "You've chosen a tough job."

"You're not kidding," he answered. "The stress that these

kids produce has caused me to lose over ten pounds in a month. I've totally lost my appetite."

"Is that so? Has she lost weight, too?" I indicate his chubby co-worker with the red hair.

"Oh, no. Just the opposite." He shakes his head. "These kids aggravate her, so she eats all day. She's gained over ten pounds since we started this job. I know because she's my girlfriend."

I have accidently proven that they both have different tipping point reactions. Everyone reacts differently to stress!

CHAPTER 12

DR. SCOTT, MY BUDDY

I arrive early for my coffee rendezvous with my good friend Scott, and I'm lucky to see him waiting for me. After a few jokes and my updating him on the happenings in my life, he volunteers that he is still single. He complains that he is over-worked every day. He admits that in the near future he will get an incredible raise that might compensate for his being overworked because he will then be able to afford a European vacation. Seeing my sad eyes, he adds, "Buddy, I'm inviting you, too."

"Impossible, mi amigo." We really are buddies and ami-gos, having been the kind of friends since kindergarten who never fail to keep in touch. During our lives, we've shared many adventures together.

I produced the questions I had prepared. "Why does anxiety cause weight loss? Can stress cause weight loss even when eating?"

"I'll answer your second question first. Since cortisol is a stress-hormone stimulant, higher levels of cortisol can cause the body to work harder, which can cause an increase in fuel consumption. Now if the stress response is over-stimulated, the response decreases the body's ability to absorb nutrients from the food. Reduced nutrition causes weight loss, understand? Actually, I answered both questions with that answer.

"Now ask me how to get rid of weight loss symptoms. First, reduce body stress as much as possible, which will reduce fuel consumption and weight loss. Second, slow down the body's metabolism by relaxing. Good sleeping habits will also lower fuel consumption. Third, increase your food intake to offset the higher demand for fuel. Fourth, take a nutritional supplement if needed. Fifth, look for an endocrinologist or a nutritional therapist. They know how to help with this problem."

Our hour was nearly up. Before leaving, he hugged me and volunteered to help with the medical end of my project.

CHAPTER 13

KIM THE VOLUNTEER IS READY

Kim is on time. We decide to go to Hotel Tortuga on 14th Street because they serve tacos, burritos, and breakfast-all-day, and I want a cheese omelet. After we're seated and order, Kim hands me his resumé.

Surprised, I ask, "Why? I'm not hiring you."

"I know. I just want to impress you with my curriculum vitae," he says. "I'm an expert in communication, and from the little you've told me, you'll need an assistant."

"Thank you, Kim. You're right, I could use an assistant. But I don't have any money to pay you. This is my first job, and it's a summer job with a low salary."

Kim smiles. "I'm not looking to be paid, Mitch. I just want to help with the project. Mere participation will give me added knowledge and incredible experience. I'll meet new people and maybe make new friends."

I can tell that with his positive attitude, Kim is going to be useful. I start outlining my plan. "I think I have the overweight volunteer, but I am not 100% sure because I haven't asked her yet. You're my skinny volunteer, and I'm going to participate as the normal-weight person. If I can find an overweight and an underweight person from thirteen to fifteen years old to volunteer, I will attempt to use the data obtained in our experiment with them."

"And I'll prepare an Excel program so we can keep the input as scientific as possible, and I'll enter the data every day. I'll also develop a way to allow us to transmit all the information about what and how much food we consume, and how much we gain and lose."

"Great. Getting the teenagers to be conscientious may be difficult, though."

"Not if they have an iPhone. I know an app that makes everything easy. The question is, how are we going to reward the participants?"

I can't answer immediately. "Don't you think that the satisfaction from participating in an incredible experiment and from being mentioned in the media articles that will result is reward in itself?"

"For me it will be, but I can't speak for the other participants."

"Of course, they'll also be mentioned in the book I'll write. And after we have the results, they'll have resolved their problems—you'll have resolved yours, too, Kim. You're going to embark on a self-imposed overeating diet followed by a difficult attempt to lose the excess pounds. I'm glad that you feel the added knowledge and experience make the process worth it. My satisfaction will come from proving my theories and maybe landing a permanent job with *The Daily Flash*— not to mention that the experiment will give me a subject for my first book. And most important are the great friends that we'll make by the end of this incredible journey." Kim nods, and I take a bite of my omelet before continuing.

"You know, Kim, I only graduated one month ago. I had no idea what I was going to do. I applied for a summer job and got it. Now here I am, seven days later, full of ideas and heading a small team of volunteers whom I found by accident in this crazy world. All of a sudden I feel like I have a purpose, a calling to make changes by gathering useful information that will better society. This experiment can be a stimulus to positive change in people's lives." I put my fork down and lean toward Kim. "I'm so lucky to have met you, Kim. You are my one gigantic asset. I hope we're successful— what am I saying? I know we'll be successful."

"Your words inspire me, Mitch. Although we've only just met, after listening to your project and its goals, you have awakened a special *adventuresque* feeling within me. I'm all go with you. Let's get together with your volunteers and establish a workable program—and I think I can help you find those two young kids. Give me a day or two. I will inquire among my church group."

"Great, Kim. I'll also search on my own."

"Right now I want to add some more hot sauce to this veggie burrito."

"I'll keep myself light with this succulent egg and cheese omelet." I smile. "Kim, you're heaven-sent."

Kim considers this possibility as he replaces the cap on the tabasco bottle. "Yes, maybe," he says with a grin.

CHAPTER 14

SHIRLEY'S CALL

After leaving Kim, I notice that I missed a call from Shirley. She left a message saying that she needs to talk with me urgently. I decide to text her before entering the subway: OK meet U @ Starbucks @ 8.

On the way, I check my new email account that I created to find possible tenants with whom to share my apartment. The inbox is full with over 100 messages! Some come with pictures attached, others with CVs. Some are from men, others are from women. From some, I can't decide what the gender is. Some letters are hilarious, others downright obscene. I could write a book entitled *The Consequences of Listing an Apartment on Craigslist*. I decide to read the more serious responses and delete the rest.

Before getting off the subway, I've narrowed the responses to three. I decide to see if they'll meet me at Union Square's Strand bookstore where I love to browse. The Strand is by far the best bookstore that I've ever visited. I send each of them an e-mail scheduling them to meet me one hour apart near the arts section. I advise them that I'll be wearing a green shirt emblazoned with the Statue of Liberty so they can easily identify me.

Shirley is waiting, coffee in hand. When she sees me, her eyes light up. Her smile is radiant and contagious. She gives me the feeling that she wants to hug me to death.

After she lets me sit down with my cup of coffee, she says that she has something important to tell me. All at once I get the feeling I had sex with her last night—which of course I didn't—but I feel she is going to tell me, *Honey, we're pregnant*. What goes through people's minds is incredible.

"Mitch, you won't believe what I've decided." Her eyes sparkle as she clasps my hands. "I want to volunteer for your experiment." She speaks with so much energy that it seems like this decision is an accomplishment. "I'll be totally successful, I guarantee it," she continues. "And I'm the type of person who means what I say."

I can feel her determination. Every word reverberates with an enthusiasm unknown to me. All I can do is hug her, grateful for her decision, and say, "Welcome to the team." I launch into an elaborate description of everything I've done and everyone I've met. I describe the established goals and timetables.

"I can be of total help. I have as much time as you need. My regular schedule doesn't begin for over three months. All I do all day or whenever I want is practice my music—now that I'm starting to compose on my own. So I'm free. Please let me help."

I know that I'm going to finally create *a fat man's dream*— a way to lose weight and keep it off. We continue to talk and plan until Starbucks closes.

CHAPTER 15

DAY FOUR

Alexa is great! She never forgets to wake me up on time. Before Alexa, I was late for everything. In reality, this is the first time that I've had a paying job, so I shouldn't only credit Alexa for my successful on-time awaking. Getting a paycheck is a good motivator. Still, this Amazon product is the best.

Esperanza is as jolly as ever as she accepts her *cortadito* with unusual grace. She asks me to lean near and whispers, "Mitch, I'm close to getting your expense money. Give me another day and I'll have it." I hug her in front of the staff, so everyone stares at us. I feel like playing one of Juan Luis Guerras' songs so Esperanza and I can dance while everyone applauds our incredible and sensual moves. But, of course, I haven't conquered everyone's friendship, so I quiet down. I nod to all the observers and leave for the day—after checking in with Mr. Petro, of course.

CHAPTER 16

THE STRAND

head to a nearby Whole Foods Market where I grab a Danish and coffee and then hurry to The Strand to prepare to meet my future roommate. The Strand is always full of people. I enjoy browsing in all bookstores, but The Strand is special. They advertise that their NYC bookstore is the legendary home of eighteen miles of new, used, and rare books—and I believe them. Eighty-six-year-old Fred Bass remains the co-owner and he still works at the store. He loves to boast that over 2.5 million books fill the shelves.

Precisely at 10 a.m. the first candidate arrives. At 6'9" George is a tall fellow with an elongated neck and a face full of freckles. He's twenty-seven and the friendly type. He tells me that he has just landed a summer job at the Bronx Zoo, but that he loves the area where the rental is located. He was an ornithology major at a southern university. When I ask him why he has a camera around his neck, he explains, "I'm always on the lookout for birds. You never know when you're going to spot a strange species." This seems strange, but then I realize that that's how ornithologists think.

I explain all the duties and obligations that I require. When I tell him that he will have to sleep on a rollaway sofa, he hesitates because of his height. To sleep with his feet sticking out would be uncomfortable.

"Could I bring my own sleeping pad?"

"I have several other candidates to interview, so I'll contact you if I choose you."

"I'll abide by all your rules," George persists. "Finding a three-month rental is so hard." When I say nothing, he blurts, "I'll be useful, too. I love to cook, and I'll—I'll cook for you at no cost." Now this is definitely an incentive.

"How do you keep in such good shape?" I ask.

"I'm a motivational trainer. In Memphis, Tennessee, where I'm from, I worked my way through college in a hi-tech gym every night from six to nine." When he sees how interested I've become, he adds, "I've successfully helped over a 100 private clients manage their exercise and training. I even belong to a bariatric group that meets on weekends. I've been able to really help these guys." With that I change my decision and put him at the top of the list of possible candidates.

To my surprise, the second candidate is a woman. Since she hadn't included a picture in her e-mail, I had assumed that Leslie was a man. Come to think of it, both sexes use that name.

Leslie is a beautiful redhead, thinner than Kim, and very impressive. She has a summer job in Manhattan, and she just arrived two hours ago from Michigan where she studied industrial design in Ann Arbor. She must be twenty-one or close to it .When she smiles, dimples form on her cheeks. To look at her is really pleasant.

"Won't you mind sharing a very small apartment with me—a sexually active male?"

Without missing a beat she says, "No problem for me if it's no problem for you." That was one helluva cool answer.

"I've narrowed the list of the hundred who answered my Craigslist advertisement down to three."

"So what made you choose me?"

"You're a senior in a profession that I wanted to study, but I never could make up my mind. Now I'm a journalist who just started his first job. I'd definitely consider you."

"Come on, Mitch. You know you're never going to get a clean, orderly, efficient roommate like me. You need to decide now. Don't postpone."

My radar kicks in. Leslie is desperate.

"To be truthful, I don't know anyone in New York City, and I don't have anywhere to stay tonight. I have very little money, so I can't afford to stay in a hotel. But as soon as I start my job, they'll give me a daily allowance besides my salary."

I understand her dilemma. Without thinking, I say, "No problem, Leslie. Tonight you can stay with me. Just let me interview my last candidate, and then I'll give you a definite answer. Wait for me in the coffee shop on the corner."

The next candidate is standing right next to me.

Apparently he arrived early and identified me because of my green shirt. I realize that he has probably overheard some of my exchange with Leslie.

"Hi," he says. "Are you Mitch?" I nod, and he continues. "I'm Marcello, your twelve o'clock appointment. Sorry, but I overheard your conversation with that gorgeous gal. I assume there's no need to interview me because this girl has to have conquered the space in your apartment."

"What makes you so sure?"

"Mitch, my friend, you look like a man who goes for women. If this one didn't make you decide, than you're not the type of man I think you are. She's fabulous!"

"True, but let me interview you, anyway." I'd taken a close look at this guy, and he was as telegenic as you can get, meaning he'd look great on TV. Believe me, I'm straight—a woman's man, not a man's, but I needed a guy like that on my team. "So, Marcello, your CV says that you're in the City for a temporary job with NBC, and that you just graduated from UCLA as a journalist."

"That's right."

"Well, that's why I want to interview you. I'm also a recent journalism grad, and I just landed my first temporary job at a local newspaper. I'm working on a special project, and I thought that perhaps a guy like you could help me."

"Hey, accept me as your roommate, and you can take it for granted that I'll help you."

"All right, Marcello. Give him a little time to think things over."

I had just created one heck of a problem for myself. George the ornithologist would be immensely helpful as a cook and a motivational trainer for my team of volunteers. Leslie the Industrial Engineer was one helluva catch, but, most importantly, I could use her as a volunteer for my project by having her gain some additional pounds as part of the team with Kim. This Marcello could also be a positive asset. He's attractive and imposing and he has the type of personality that easily gets what he wants. His specialty is TV. My research before, during and after the experiment could benefit from a video account, and I know Marcello could achieve this objective. So how the hell am I going to get the three of them in Carol's apt?

I decide to take a gamble and talk to Kim and Shirley to see if they'd be willing to take in one of the three. I'll try to get Shirley to take Leslie—*how I'd love to shack up with a woman like that! But business first; I don't need more complication.* I'm sure Kim will agree to have George stay with him, especially since George really wants to get involved with the project.

I was never a gambler. This is my first experience as a man with a mission, and I need to make decisions without ifs, ands, or buts. I walk up to Marcello with a thumbs up gesture and shake his hand. Then we go to the coffee shop where I hug Leslie in anticipation of our adventure together. Marcello also hugs her, and then I introduce them. We sit down, and I explain everything to both of them. Then I call George and tell him to meet me at Shirley's Starbucks at four.

I do the same with Shirley. Kim says he will take off early and be there.

I am definitely in business. My strategy is starting to take shape. I have a bunch of great volunteers, so I splurge by inviting Leslie and Marcello to a nearby Boston Market for a lunch special. Marcello offers to split the bill with me. Leslie doesn't attempt to contribute. When she goes to wash her hands, I explain to Marcello that she is temporarily short on money.

CHAPTER 17

OUR FIRST MEETING

We all arrive at Starbucks almost simultaneously. We appropriate a long table for six and buy coffees, and I start what is to be the real beginning of my experiment. I speak briefly with Shirley about her taking Leslie in as a roommate, and she accepts without hesitation. When I introduce Shirley to Marcello, she acts like she did when she first met me. She's probably deciding that if she loses weight, she has a chance with him and men like us in general. Kim is also positive and approves of taking George in as a border.

"Well, dear new friends and now allies in this experiment, I want you all to know that I have hired you to participate and work gratis for what may turn out to be of aid to the many worldwide who struggle with eating problems and their health consequences. I have given each of you an idea of my plan. Three of you responded to an advertisement because you needed a temporary place to live in this great and very expensive borough of Manhattan. I enticed you to join me, and I'm sure you will not regret your decision. In the end, we will all benefit. I'm not talking about economic benefit, but benefits from having contributed to helping people in need of assistance with their weight problems.

"I want to introduce you to Shirley. This beautiful woman is extremely motivated to lose sufficient weight in the next ten weeks to make an exemplary difference. Shirley is a future star in the musical composing and recording industry. She will be successful in whatever she does, I'm sure." I turn to Kim.

"Here is Kim, an incredible technology engineer who works in the print industry. He will attempt, this time successfully, to gain sufficient weight to make him happy with his image—no irony intended.

"Now I want to introduce you to the three persons I met today. George is an ornithologist and a motivational trainer with several successes to his credit. He will help us train all the volunteers in losing and gaining pounds to reach their goals." Kim stands and asks to speak.

"Mitch, I have recruited a new volunteer who is obese and wants to join the program. I'm sure Wallis will be an asset to our group."

"Great job, Kim. Now we have two fat subjects and two skinny ones, so we are protected if one quits. If no one quits, our statistics will be more reliable. I would also like to mention that Kim is knowledgeable about programs and will maintain all the high-tech data on the four participants—and on me, of course. I have decided not to look for young children as originally planned due to the time factor as well as the difficulty in controlling data at that age level.

"I now would like to introduce Leslie, another beautiful woman whose problem is the exact opposite of Shirley's. Leslie and Shirley will be roommates. Leslie is a highly-organized future industrial design specialist who will contribute all her knowledge.

"And last but not least, as the saying goes, here is Marcello. A successful future is assured for this handsome and able journalist. Marcello will help with videography and photography to record the advancements in our experiment. He will redact the documentary report that my employer, *The Daily Flash*, will publish. You should also know that I am being assisted by a physician, Dr. Scott, and a psychologist, Kathy. In addition, we can count on the newspaper's head secretary, Esperanza Delgado. Furthermore, Dr. Scott's uncle, Marvin, is overweight, and he may help us by sharing his stories. Marvin has attempted every diet known and will speak about the pros and cons pertaining to our area of interest. Any questions?"

CHAPTER 18

THE QUESTIONS

M arcello starts the questioning. "Mitch, doesn't the data to your experiment already exist? I mean, have you searched the Internet? A million serious sites deal with the problems you're trying to explore. Why complicate things with a complex series of investigative details? Why not just research the subject and publish your newspaper article? I'm sure Kim here would appreciate it. He's going to be the one with one helluva workload."

Kim rises. "I understand your concerns, Marcello, and your questions are excellent. In answering them, I hope to help the group understand Mitch's' innovative idea on this subject. Mitch will have two very fat volunteers who will dedicate the next ten weeks to doing everything known and maybe unknown to lose weight in an orderly and programmed way that won't harm their health.

"This weight loss will take into account their ages, environments, and the stimuli for their decision to lose weight.

They are going into this program with the goal of keeping the weight off and not doing what the majority of programs cause, which is return to overeating.

"The same applies to Leslie and me. We will attempt to gain pounds until we reach a normal weight, which obviously we have not been successful in doing.

"But the most innovative feature of this experiment is that Mitch, who is of normal weight, will indulge in extreme overeating for the first month, and for the second month, will attempt to lose the weight he's gained.

"All the data that we accumulate will be fresh, so we hope to derive innovative conclusions. All the information will be available and will serve as a guide for what to do and what not to do to achieve success. I think it's a fantastic idea."

Mitch stands. "Thank you, Kim, for your very clear exposition. I couldn't have explained it better!"

George raises a finger. "Will I be needed to cook for the five involved in the diets?"

"This would be a good idea," Leslie says, "because we need to keep accurate data of everything so there are no scientific blurs. I understand that you have a job at the Bronx Zoo. Will you have the time?"

"I do work at the zoo. I'm in charge of making sure that the zoo's food shopping is health-oriented for all the animals. But that only takes two hours a day, so I'm free the rest of the day, and I'm totally free on weekends. What's your summer job, Leslie?"

"I'll be working with an architectural firm. I don't know

what my obligations will be yet, but don't worry. I'm a work-alcoholic, so I'll find time for everything. I love the idea of this plan."

Shirley turns to Kim. "When can we meet your friend Wallis? I need to see him and feel his aura!" Everyone smiles, and Marcello stands to congratulate the team.

"I'm impressed. I now believe this plan is a great idea, and I'm with you." We decide to meet at a Whole Foods Market for a quick dinner.

As the others prepare to leave, Shirley leans in and whispers, "Will the presence of Leslie and the rest of the group alter our relationship?"

"Shirley, the exact opposite will happen," I say, hugging her. "Besides analyzing what is happening, you are fundamental and the initiator of my plan."

CHAPTER 19

DAY FIVE

*A*lexa, what time is it?
6:15 a.m.
I get up early. I guess there's a lot of excitement in the air—in my air. I fix up the apt, readying it for Marcello who is to move in at 7 a.m. I have many questions, and I go through them in my mind, mostly the ones about food.

Am I going to have to contribute to food shopping? Will the volunteers have to come to Kim's apartment to pick up the food? I assume Kim will agree to George's cooking at his place. Maybe Leslie will be in charge of the food delivery system.

I need to get everyone together this weekend to formulate the guidelines and regulations for this experiment. Where can we meet? The place has to have quiet. We are nine—assuming that Esperanza, Dr. Scott, and Kathy can assist.

Will Marcello stay positive, or will he be a constant critic?

Can I keep my eyes and urges under control? That Leslie is such a tease, or maybe she's naturally a tease to all men, not only me. Marcello, George, and Kim also went out of their minds when they first saw her. I have to be careful with Shirley. She can't suspect that I feel like being all over Leslie. In fact, Shirley is the only reason why I didn't choose Leslie as my roommate—especially after she said she didn't mind living in the same apartment with a sex-crazed guy like me. Marcello thought I was crazy. Or gay. Regardless, I have to keep focused. I'm the initiator, the leader, and totally responsible for the results and consequences of this experiment. Whether I'm a success or failure, my future is at stake.

Marcello appears at the apartment with a backpack. He organizes his assigned portion of the small room and leaves for his first day at work.

I arrive at *The Daily Flash* with *cortadito* in hand, and Esperanza is glowing. She indicates that Mr. Petro needs to talk with me. Whatever the reason, from her expression it looks like good news. I relax as she escorts me into Mr. Petro's office and has me sit while he finishes his phone call.

Mr. Petro is pleasant and in a good mood. The phone conversation seems to have been with his wife. Esperanza resists leaving after he thanks her and indicates that she can go.

Esperanza smiles. "I would rather stay."

Mr. Petro pulls another chair close to his desk for her. "Okay, Esperanza. You always get what you want." He turns to me. "Mitch, I am going to make $25,000 available for your expenses. We'll give you a debit card, and Esperanza will keep track of the account. Receipts are mandatory for every cent you spend."

"Thank you so much," was all I could say—and at that moment I notice that Petro and Esperanza have something going on. He looks at her in a manner that indicates *I gave you what you want; now you have to give me what I want*—or so I think. Well, this is none of my business, but I'm quick to take advantage of this magic moment as they gaze at each other with a special type of sensuality.

"Is there any chance that my project volunteers and I could use the conference room over the weekend?"

They both nod. Mr. Petro smiles and says, "Certainly. Whatever you want."

Esperanza stands and moves to his side of the desk, warmly thanking him. I leave the room, closing the door behind me, to give her a chance to thank him properly.

Esperanza is going to be a huge asset to my project. I leave a note on her desk:

Dear Esperanza,

You are great!

Do you have time to attend a meeting with my group?

We will be here at 10 a.m. this Saturday in the newspaper's conference room.

Thank you!
Mitch

CHAPTER 20

BACK TO HOFSTRA

head straight to Penn Station. I want to get back to my room in Hempstead and retrieve the rest of my belongings before they close down for the summer. The Long Island train is always on time, and, by chance, I meet one of my journalism instructors, Mr. Bayley.

I tell him about my job and work plan. He is so proud of everything I tell him that he asks me to accompany him to Hofstra's cafeteria for a coffee and tell him more. We arrange to meet at one p.m.

When I return to my alma mater, I realize that I am really going to miss this school. I've spent the best moments of my life here. I plan one day to get a masters in some specialty, but that means more tuition for which I simply do not have the funds. I can always write to my Uncle Sam who promised to help me economically if I ever became really desperate, but I've never been that desperate yet.

Uncle Sam is the only one of my father's brothers who

never married. He made his money in the real estate market. Uncle Sam used to love to travel with us. I love him, and I'm his favorite nephew. (At least, that's what he tells people when I'm around.) He always remembers my birthday, and since he's the only uncle who does, I don't forget his, either.

I pick up the mail and find an envelope from Uncle Sam— probably a graduation card. I'll open it later. I need to get rid of so much junk.

It takes me two hours to leave the room in decent condition. I pick up what is useful and walk to the LIRR station and place the bags in a locker. Then I rush to the bus that takes me to the library where I spot Mr. Bayley with two other department instructors.

They greet me warmly since Mr. Bayley has told them about my proposed plan, and they offer to collaborate if needed. They have incredible vitaes citing affiliations with top USA news agencies and national networks. I'll tell you, they elevate my ego, and that's a psychological positive. They make me feel like one of them, like a colleague.

CHAPTER 21

GEORGE'S THOUGHTS

When I got the job at the zoo, I was happy because it's in Manhattan. I visited the city when I was thirteen, but I was never able to return. I had such great expectations for what I would find here, and so far my experiences are exceeding those expectations.

All of a sudden I'm part of an experimental group. All of a sudden I have friends in New York City! I can work at the zoo for pocket money, and I'm about to have a new chance training people who need to lose weight. I'll also gain culinary experience cooking for my group of newfound friends.

Kim is a really super-bright young man, and he, too, is majorly excited about this project. Although we know we're embarking on a difficult undertaking, with Mitch's incredible leadership we're confident that we'll be successful.

Because I'm so tall, I've always had difficulty meeting new friends and sleeping over anywhere. Getting into small cars has always been a pain in the neck—literally and figuratively.

I'm lucky that Kim has a long sofa where I can sleep comfortably. That Leslie is one hell of a girl. I'm going to love working closely with her. Her beauty and personality are infectious.

CHAPTER 22

LESLIE'S THOUGHTS

My expectations have been achieved. I was scared as hell when, two days ago, I got the call offering me a job in Manhattan. I had already accepted a job at a teenage summer camp, so, of course, I had to call and explain to the camp manager why I had to renege. A job in Manhattan? That's the dream of a girl like me—let alone a job within my field. And at $2000 a month? The reality is too much to believe.

My funds are so low that I had to borrow money from my roommate for the airline ticket. My parents are divorced, and they have serious economic debts. My father is a good guy, but whenever he makes some money, he gambles it away. That's why they divorced. He and my mother are so involved with their problems that I couldn't even reach them to let them know about my New York job. I'm an only child, so I don't have siblings to fall back on.

Because my mom is beautiful, all the men want to hang

out with her, and she always chooses the wrong kind. I'm lucky to look like Mom, but we have the same problem. We're extremely thin. Although I try, I can't seem to gain weight.

I've had a lucky streak, though. When I wrote the e-mail answering the ad about the apartment rental, I was at the airport getting ready to board the New York flight. As soon as I arrived at La Guardia, I had an email from Mitch. We met just two hours later at The Strand, an amazing bookstore. I also met another incredible member of the group, Marcello, who is something. I have to be careful with two difficult men to juggle since I'm aware that everyone perceives my sensuality whether I want them to or not.

I feel really good with the group. I must admit, Shirley is extraordinary. She's so lively and caring, and she has a tremendous personality. She demonstrated her ability with her harmonica and banjo, and I just know she'll become a famous celebrity. She'll also be special physically when she achieves her weight expectation.

I was delighted to discover that although small, Shirley's apartment is gorgeous.

CHAPTER 23

MARCELLO'S PLAN

W hen NBC called me to be master of ceremonies for a new music program, I had to cancel all my contractual appearances in Los Angeles. Having participated as a standby for various television programs, I was well-known in LA. But when you're only twenty-four years old and a major network calls and you owe a fortune in education loans, you accept immediately.

I still don't know exactly what NBC wants me to do. The producer who called told me to get to New York immediately and report to the NBC studio at 9 a.m. on Friday.

I'm also lucky to have responded to an ad and gotten a cheap shared-apartment near Central Park, which I love. My roommate Mitch is cool, a born leader. I can't believe he chose me to share the place with him. His friend Leslie, who is one helluva piece of ass despite being skinny, was willing to room with Mitch, but he didn't choose her, which I can't understand. I'm considered a macho man and few girls refuse my company, so for a moment there I thought Mitch must be gay. My roommate in LA was gay and a great guy—but Mitch isn't gay.

I really dig this group, and I will definitely do what Mitch suggests. I feel he has a good vibe. He's my type of man, and I like him. I also like Leslie and the rest of the group. I'll be as collaborative as possible.

CHAPTER 24

FRIDAY AFTERNOON

I call all the members of my group and inform them about the Saturday 10 o'clock meeting at *The Daily Flash*. Then I call Dr. Scott and Kathy, and they also say they'll be there. I feel like company tonight, so I ask Shirley to dine with me. We are to meet at our usual place.

The truth is that I'm tired of eating on the run, so I go to a local market and buy a large can of anchovies, six beers, three French baguettes, some babaganush and hummus, and return home. I call Shirley again and tell her to come over and bring some soda. I leave the door open and fall asleep.

Shirley wakes me with a kiss to my forehead. She looks exquisite, and I tell her so. She loves that observation and hugs me until I can't breathe. (She is strong—very strong.) I open a soda for Shirley and a beer for me, and we're ready to start our feast when Leslie walks in.

"Hey, welcome," I say. Shirley had texted her, and Leslie

had responded that she had nowhere to go, so Shirley told her to come by.

Leslie takes over serving the food. "I'm starving," she says.

The anchovies with the hummus spread are delightful. We have a great time eating and laughing and getting better acquainted. Ten minutes later Marcello calls. I have not given him a key yet and he needs to come and change. I tell him I'm home, so he comes right over. His dinner engagement isn't until 9 p.m., so he has time for a beer with us.

I ask Alexa to play some Juan Jose Luis Guerra songs, and we start to dance to his fine merengue music. Guerra is by far my favorite Latin singer. Marcello tells us that he met Guerra in Guerra's hometown of Santo Domingo in the Dominican Republic where he saw Guerra in a concert performance that he said was out of this world.

I dance with my two ladies. It's good that I've had only two beers because if I were a little higher, I don't know if I could control my instincts in this incredibly sensual environment.

Marcello rushes off to dinner, and I fall asleep.

The girls probably went to their apartment.

CHAPTER 25

DAY SIX

'd programmed Alexa to wake me at 6:30 a.m. Marcello had come back late, so I let him sleep until just before I left at 9 a.m.. I'd asked Shirley if she would take the subway to Costco on East 117th and buy a pack of their fabulous croissants. My group has made plans to arrive early.

Esperanza is at the newspaper office when I arrive. Since I didn't know if she would be there, I didn't bring the daily cortadito. She is in her usual lovable mood and has prepared hot coffee for everyone. She turns to me. "Mitch, would you mind if Petro attends?" She blushes, which makes me understand that this is her wish, so I answer affirmatively.

Immediately she texts him. *Mr Petro your assistance at Mitch's meeting is required.* She is happy and shows it. She whispers, although no one else has arrived, "Mr. Petro's wife is a tramp. She treats him terribly, so I don't want him to be in his house when he can be with me." In her regular voice she adds, "He really is a good man."

As the group arrives, Scott calls in to tell me he will be late. He wants to visit one of his sick patients at the hospital. He has empathy and is one hell of a doctor.

I fuel up my team with the coffee and croissants since I'm sure they've not had breakfast. "So this is the program," I begin. "Monday is D-day—the beginning of the experiment. Since you're all busy, the four participating in the special diets and I will need to pick up your planned meals at Kim's apartment. Kathy, who just arrived—" I nod at Kathy as she takes her seat and reaches for a croissant, "—is a psychologist and knowledgeable about nutrition. She and George will implement food strategies particularly for the two fat and two skinny volunteers. Welcome, Kathy." Kathy smiles and nods to the group. "I will not participate in the ready-food system that Kim and Leslie are going to prepare because, for the first five weeks, I'm going to be going crazy and overeating on all the junk food I can find. However, I will participate in the last five weeks."

I turn to the person seated on my right. "Mr. Perry Petro and Wallis, please stand and meet our team. Welcome to your solution group. Mr. Petro is my boss. His personal secretary is Esperanza—" I nod in her direction, "—who is and will be fabulous with our team. I want to thank Mr. Petro who just donated a generous sum for our immediate expenses."

Everyone applauds. "Esperanza receives a cortadito from me every morning," I continue, "and she has reciprocated by offering us this delicious coffee. The croissants are compliments of Shirley, who got up bright and early to take the subway to Costco on the other side of town to buy them."

More applause follows for Shirley. At that moment Dr. Scott arrives, apologizing for his tardiness. "Since you all have smartphones," I continue, "we will form a WhatsApp group so we can update all our data and share information and instructions. With his tech abilities, Kim will be responsible for keeping everything in order. Esperanza has volunteered to receive calls to resolve any personal problems you may encounter. Mr. Petro has also said that we can count on him. Our friend Marcello will be recording the conversations and using video whenever he thinks it will contribute to the scientific value of our experiment.

"If you have any medical questions, please don't hesitate to contact Dr. Scott. He'll take care of everything within his scope. Leslie and Kim will be in charge of purchasing food with Kathy as their guide."

"I can also help in that department," Dr. Scott interjected.

"George will be our chef, and I will, of course, be available to all of you 24/7. This may sound like an overload of work and functions, but successful people find the time to get everything done even when they don't have time. I've selected you because I feel you are the type of leaders I need, and I welcome all of you to this volunteer experiment.

"Now I'm going to share some data that I found on the Internet. After, we'll have a thirty minute break so you can all get to know each other better. Today we've become a team. Let's call ourselves the Body Shapers Dream Team.

"According to the Centers for Disease Control and Prevention (CDC), 155 million Americans are overweight. While exercise is critical for good health, the CDC says that exercise is not a reliable way to keep off body fat over the long term. The overly-simplistic arithmetic of calories in vs calories out has given way to a more nuanced understanding: What sustains weight loss is the composition of the person's diet rather than how much a person burns off working out. The CDC also explain that the best diet for one person is likely not the best diet for his neighbor. The response to different diets, from low-fat and vegan to low-carb and paleo, is individual and varies significantly from person to person. Some individuals lose sixty pounds on a diet and keep those pounds off for two years. Others on the same diet who follow all the instruction gain five pounds. In other words, a highly personalized diet versus a trendy one is recommended. As we all know, dieting is not easy—and our plan of action is not easy. But we will use our short term results, over ten weeks, to demonstrate what we can achieve with our plan. Researchers have noted that people on long-term weight loss systems tend to be motivated not by a slimmer waist, but rather by a health scare or by the desire to live longer and be able to spend more time with their loved ones. One thing will be clear at the end of our experiment: Your lives and mine will be better."

After the mingling session ends, I feel lucky to have found and formed a team that exceeds my expectations. These people mean business. Furthermore, they're motivated without an expectation of monetary gain, which is unusual these days.

When it's time to leave, I am to meet individually with Scott and Kathy concerning the different diets for the skinny and fat, but when the group asks why we don't all leave together for Central Park and enjoy each other's company, I can't refuse. The day is spectacular, and we've worked over six hours straight. Scott reminds us that we haven't eaten and suggests a pizza party. Shirley has her guitar and Wallis offers to sing.

"For those of you who can't come today," I say, "we'll have a working picnic tomorrow morning in East River State Park. Please bring your own food." We all leave the building with joyous enthusiasm. Esperanza and Mr. Petro excuse themselves and wish us a great day.

CHAPTER 26

DAY SEVEN

Alexa is not programmed to awaken me on Sundays, so I wake up late—after nine. I awaken Marcello and we rush to a nearby farmers market to buy food for the picnic. Today the weather promises to be excellent, so we want to take advantage of every moment.

Everyone enjoyed yesterday afternoon's party. Scott brought pizzas for everyone, and Kim brought water. Shirley played her guitar and accompanied newcomer Wallis whose voice is like Sinatra's; he's really good. Marcello told him he wants to represent him, and that he'll introduce him to some guy he knows in the business. My team has reached synchronization mode. Everyone has become everyone else's friend and mentor.

East River State Park in Williamsburg, Brooklyn is not fancy, but I chose it because the view of Manhattan is breathtaking. By midday, we have all arrived. We find a shaded area where we can sit and talk.

Kim initiates the conversation with Kathy, Scott, and George about the two different diets and their contents. Leslie and George have to leave by three to reach a nearby Sunday Farm Sale where they can buy wholesale organic ingredients. Kim has an incredible kitchen outfitted with all the necessary cooking gadgets. The take-out containers need to be bought. Since Kim wants the bookkeeping job, Esperanza, who is in charge of the cards accounting, gives him the debit card.

Scott has listed a preliminary series of meal ideas for the thin group, while Kathy has spent hours preparing a reasonable menu for the fat group. Lists are being made, e-mails and WhatsApp messages are being sent. Everyone is busy working as a group. Shirley and Wallis have become friends and are trading ideas and concerns. They are preparing the picnic ingredients for quick consumption as soon as the group is ready.

This creative work environment glows with a special aura that everyone appreciates. Marcello initiates a video called *The Body Shapers Dream Team* that he plans on turning into a documentary on the new group. He continually takes pictures and films, interviews the team, and records their conversations. He resembles a famous film director and cameraman in one. No one is idle. Each has one or more roles and obligations.

Esperanza comes by to check on us and prepares delicious coffee. She asks if we need anything else. Uncle Marvin wasn't invited because of his mobility problem. (He needs a friendly bathroom nearby, and this park doesn't have one.)

After we eat, Shirley and Wallis initiate a medley with songs from the Carpenters. The lyrics to "We've Only Just Begun" are perfect:

> "We've only just begun to live
> White laces and promises
> A kiss for luck and we're on our way . . .
>
> Before the risin' sun, we fly
> So many roads to choose
> We'll start out walkin' and learn to run
> (And yes, we've just begun)"

Some leave to continue their food shopping while others decide to stay till the park closes. Shirley, Marcello and I return to our apartment for a last discussion on implementation.

CHAPTER 27

DAY EIGHT

I open my eyes before Alexa emits her wake-up signal. Today is important. Marcello will start filming at Kim's house, and I need to be present. I know that Leslie has decided to stay overnight at Kim's so they can cook until late. At 9 a.m. today she starts her new job, which is close to Kim's apartment.

I weigh myself at a nearby CVS pharmacy. I am my usual 154 lbs. I go to McDonald's and order their most caloric breakfast. Then I order a malted sundae and two large fries. I wash everything down with a coffee with double cream and three sugars. I note my consumption information and send it to Kim's app. I have never eaten so much breakfast in my life. In no time I'm searching for a bathroom. I find out that after eating heavily, I have to be near a bathroom because like a goose, I evacuate after every meal.

I reach Kim's apartment where, to my surprise, I find most of the team assembled. Kathy and Scott are having coffee. I immediately visualize them as an item. In fact they have on the same clothes they wore at yesterday's picnic. Kathy's hair, which is usually well-kept, is in disarray. I begin to suspect that my experiment is bringing people together for more than experimental purposes.

Shirley and Wallis arrive to pick up the day's meals. Marcello is videoing non-stop. George is late for his first day at the zoo so he excuses himself. Leslie has just come from the shower. She rushes to get dressed in something Shirley has brought for her. Kim seems tired. They must have worked late. I ensure that everything is in order and rush them to their jobs. Shirley and I stay behind to clean up the mess caused by so much food preparation.

Shirley grabs her portions and we go to Starbucks to sit and talk. While I buy us coffee, she takes out her prepared breakfast bag.

Scott told me that he and Kathy spent several hours planning their low calorie, low carbohydrate, 85% protein meals. In applying principals they learned in nutrition, they modified the contents according to the latest findings. Researchers say that the key to weight loss appears to be highly personalized rather than the generic trendy diets. Eating fewer calories should make a person lose weight, but when a person loses weight, resting metabolism slows down, so the person gains the weight back. As a person re-gains lost weight, the resting metabolism doesn't speed up, so the person gains weight faster than before dieting.

With this knowledge, researchers show that re-gaining weight isn't just a lack of willpower, but that biology makes long-term weight loss difficult. Yet, despite biology, many people are able to lose weight on any diet. So weight loss and gain vary from person to person. The same solution cannot resolve weight problems for everyone.

CHAPTER 28

MR. BAYLEY CALLS

At 10 a.m. I receive a call from my instructor Mr. Bayley who asks me if I have time to meet with him. He mentions that he is in the city and wants to introduce me to a very intelligent person. I tell him that I can meet him at noon near The Strand bookstore. He explains that the person is an Orthodox Jew who will only meet at a kosher place for coffee. He suggests Caravan of Dreams, a vegan restaurant, on East 6th Street. I accept, of course. Mr. Bayley has piqued my curiosity with this phone call. What is his objective? Well, I'll see in a little while.

I order a heavy milk shake and two pieces of chocolate cake at Starbucks. Shirley can't stop laughing at my serious attempt to accelerate my weight gain.

I rush over to *The Daily Flash* to speak with Esperanza, again without a cortadito in hand. Although it's after eleven, Mr. Petro has not arrived. Esperanza is worried because he hasn't called in to explain why he's late.

"He's never late, and he doesn't answer his phones. I know that your schedule is busy today, Mitch, so I'd booked you to see Mr. Petro at 8 a.m."

"Thanks, Esperanza. No doubt you'll hear from Mr. Petro soon." I gave her a summary of all that had happened and was about to leave when her phone rang.

"Just a moment," she says, looking at her caller ID. "It's Petro."

When she hung up, I told her I was in a hurry, but she just stared at me. "Mr Petro has discovered his wife is having an affair with an old acquaintance. He's helping her pack. She's decided to fly to Los Angeles to her mother's to calm her nerves until she decides what she wants to do."

"My God," I say. "Life is complicated."

I arrive at the kosher vegan restaurant early, so I stop at a nearby Wendy's where I consume a quarter pounder with double cheese, double fries, and a large Coke. I can't believe how tasty the combo is, or how I get it all inside me—I'm that full.

When I arrive at Caravan of Dreams, Mr. Bayley and a short, bearded man are already seated having coffee. "Rabbi, I'd like you to meet my student, Mitch Green. Mitch, this is Rabbi Zwi Trater." We shake hands and Mr. Bayley looks around saying, "Let me get our waitress to bring you a coffee."

"Oh, I'm fine," I tell him. We sit in the booth, with me facing the other two. "I already had lunch." They probably figure that I ate so I won't have to invite them to eat and then have to pay.

These feelings immediately disappear when the Rabbi says, "Please. Be my guest." I'm full, but I need to gain weight, so I order eggplant parmigiana, even though the cheese is probably soy.

The Rabbi expresses interest in my project. "Mr. Bayley was speaking with one of the directors of our synagogue who happens to be interested in the overweight problem in our community. We need your advice in this area. After you finish your summer job, we would like to hire you. We need a director and head of public relations for our community, as well as an editor for our newspaper. We pay well, and on Jewish holidays you don't work. You also get four weeks paid vacation. You have use of one of our staff apartments and one of our staff cars. You will negotiate the salary with our manager, but I can tell you that the last person to occupy the position earned over $200,000 a year."

I'm flabbergasted. This job is unbelievable.

Mr Bayley speaks up. "The Rabbi asked for a highly-motivated recent graduate, a class leader, and then you described your project. This is why I wanted you to meet Rabbi Trater."

"Do people live to eat? Or do they eat to live?" the Rabbi asks. "It seems my religion puts an extraordinary emphasis on food. Every holiday and every Shabbat, and for every ceremony, food is the main attraction. Food, food, and more food. Does God really want us eating so much? Maybe the reason is sociological. Our nation has been through so much, that perhaps we are afraid that each meal might be our last.

"We need food because the mass of food contains divine energy. That's why food contains so much power and is indispensable for life. Eating is essentially a spiritual divine experience, which means that eating is a holy experience." I have never thought of food this way.

"Take an ordinary cucumber or raisin or tomato or peach," the Rabbi continues. "Hold the food in your hand. Feel its texture. Think of where it has grown, of the sunshine, earth, and water that nourished it and is contained in it. Think of how many people are involved in getting the fruit to us: the landowners and workers, the pickers, the packaging and transportation crews. This fruit is a miracle in its creation and growth. Consider its nutritional value.

"Now that you realize what is contained in this little raisin or grape or peach, place it in your mouth and hold it there for a few seconds. Move it around. Feel it. Chew it, slowly, and experience its flavors. Then swallow it. Pause to reflect on the taste and the level of satisfaction it provides. Eating this way," he adds, "ensures that we gain maximum nourishment and enjoyment from our food while needing minimal quantities."

This man is really inspirational! I thank them both and as Rabbi Trater gets up to leave, I assure him that I will contact him once I finish my summer project. I remain with Mr. Bayley. "How can I repay you for your recommendation? I really appreciate what you did."

"That's part of the reward one receives for being good at one's profession," is his reply. "Who knows? Someday, you may be able to help me. Life constantly changes. New events continuously present themselves."

CHAPTER 29

MY THOUGHTS

Today is Day 7 in this incredible journey. I leave the restaurant with a strange feeling, like I have just finished postdoctoral programs in organizing, headhunting, speech, and now in religion. The most fascinating aspect is that I've met such wonderful people, most of whom have become devoted to me—at least, that's how I feel. They regard me as their natural leader. What's happening? What causes my magnetism? I'm incredulous that this is happening to me.

To top it off, for the first time in my life, I've met and am dealing with not one but three young women whom I like and would seriously consider dating. Shirley, Kathy, and Leslie are all women with whom I can talk and argue, women who have minds of their own, who are bright and intelligent, women whom I respect and with whom I don't have as my only objective getting them into bed.

Now how about that job offer? It's God-sent. How can a thoughtful guy recommend me for such a serious job—and one that pays over $200K? That's difficult to believe. Most graduates are lucky to land a job that pays $40K. The super-lucky ones start with $60K.

I check my special Craigslist account and see another batch of e-mails from people searching for places to stay for the ten-week summer season. I envision the universe of people I could attract by just placing a simple free advertisement for a small matter. This realization causes me to imagine the hundreds of projects I could embark on with my magnetic personality.

CHAPTER 30

LESLIE'S THOUGHTS

M y first day working on this project was really fantastic compared with my job at the architectural office. At the office, my group of summer trainees (as they refer to us), received a fast introduction to what is expected of us. I am to be the office girl this week: I'll fetch coffee and mail on a call basis and carry correspondence to the office's different construction sites. The other trainees have similar menial jobs. But I can't complain. They gave us our first check for $2000, and that's reason to celebrate. They let us out early, but I can't join my fellow trainees at their beer celebration at the local bar because I need to rush to find Kim at the food market.

I decide to call Mitch and share my day with him. He's one helluva guy, a natural leader. Everyone in our new group loves him. Gosh, I have never met a guy with such an incredible personality. He's so good looking, and those eyes—they capture me. Really, I need to be near him just to get glimpses of his eyes. He's the type of guy I would easily have a fling with. I hardly know him, yet I want to be with him every moment.

I think my roommate also has romantic feelings for him. She becomes all funny and nervous when he appears. I think she got involved in this project because of him. She wants to lose weight for him. I don't blame her. I think that Esperanza and that Kathy have their eye on him, too. He could easily form a harem. If he does, I want to be part of it.

In analyzing why he gave Marcello the opportunity to join us, I concluded that he needs someone credible to offset the girls so we'll leave him alone. Marcello is a really handsome dude. He hasn't attempted to move in on me for fear of offending Mitch. That's my opinion.

Kim and George are incredible collaborators, and I really like them. I don't really know Wallis well, so I can't give my thoughts on him yet, but he sings beautifully.

I'm sure that Mitch's project will be successful. I'll certainly do my best to make it a success.

CHAPTER 31

NIGHT ACTIVITY

I receive Leslie's call, but I don't know how to interpret her information. I think she wants to meet me alone, but she has to attend to her work with Kim and George. She's happy to receive her check on her first day on the job, but the work is not what she expected. She also wants to know how I'm doing on the first day of my over-eating diet. That reminds me; I have to eat—anything that's high in calories. I tell her to call me as soon as she's finished with all her obligations, and I will tell her where I am.

First, I go to a market and buy chopped liver, a hard roll, two brownies, and a quart of whole milk. I walk to a small pedestrian park where I sit on a stool and eat everything. It's only 4 p.m., so I call George to see how his day has been.

George is happy to hear from me. He's had a great day and is heading to Kim's place to start cooking early. He only slept three hours last night. Kim and Leslie are extremely helpful. He finds the job pleasant and easy.

I start walking toward Central Park. It's hot, but I'm happy. I start planning all sorts of businesses and alternative plans. It's like thinking in front of a chess board. I try calling Marcello, but he doesn't answer, so I leave a voice message. I don't want to bother Kim. I know he has too many projects going on at the same time. So I call Wallis.

Wallis is teacher at a city college working in the summer school program. He tells me that all is well, that he has eaten only what Kim gave him.

My phone rings.

"Hi, Mitch. It's Kathy. I was wondering if there's a plan for this evening. The group could meet in Central Park for exercise practice. George is rushing with his cooking because he's going to help me train everyone. Scott called and asked if you're going to participate in the training."

I make her believe that I know what she's talking about, but I didn't know that exercise is being considered on Day One of the diet. Heck, I'm glad that the experiment is moving forward. It has developed a self-propelling motion.

Shirley answers my call. She's doing great. She's joined her school's gym program and is doing everything they expect of her.

Scott still hasn't responded to the message I left him. Since he's busy in his practice, he gave me an alternate number for the Division of Endocrinology saying, "Tell Dr. Marlene that you're my buddy, and she'll answer any questions, especially regarding underweight patients. That's her field."

I call Dr. Marlene. After I recount everything, she explains that if the body mass index is less than 18.5, the person is underweight. "A physician can also determine if a patient is underweight based on height, weight, and diet. To gain weight, patients shouldn't eat only junk food because that will not satisfy the body's needs and will harm them instead."

"So what should a person eat to gain weight and stay healthy?"

"The healthy way to gain weight is to increase calories by adding nuts, seed toppings, cheese, and sides like almonds, sunflowers seeds, fruits or whole grain, and wheat toast. Eat foods that are rich in nutrients. Consider high protein meats; they help build muscle. Choose carbohydrates like brown rice and other whole grains. Enjoy snacks, like protein bars and drinks. Eat avocados. Eat several mini meals."

"Okay. How about exercise?"

"When exercising, don't do aerobics. They work against weight gain. Do yoga and strength training. Ask your doctor for vitamins. Make sure the person has no underlying health issues causing his weight-gain problem. Underweight is caused by genetic, thyroid, and psychological problems, to name a few."

I thank her, and she promises to come with Scott to one of our meetings.

I had forgotten to check my WhatsApp messages. They plan to meet at 7:30 p.m. They've sent each other messages about their present condition, food intake, problems, and successes for the day. I send my food intake information and hurry home to fetch my shorts and proper shoes.

Scott arrives with Kathy. I feel more strongly that something is developing. Leslie is the last to arrive. We all warm up and follow our two instructors' orders.

After we finish, I find a message from my brother Matt: *Call me immediately.*

CHAPTER 32

MY FAMILY

My uncle is very ill and wants to see me. I tell Matt that tomorrow I'll take an early train to Commack. From the train station, I'll take an Uber to the hospital.

Later that evening I go to a restaurant with Marcello and eat the biggest plate of pasta possible. I go to sleep with a full stomach—something no one recommends. Leslie wants to talk, but I explain, and she understands that today is not the right time.

Alexa awakens me with Sandra Dee's music as instructed. I get dressed and go straight to the Long Island Railroad station to catch the 6:30 a.m. train to Commack. I arrive in just over an hour and a half due to some delays. Once there, I call for an Uber and get one really fast.

Since the hospital won't allow visitors until 9 a.m. I go to the cafeteria and text my brother to meet me there. Then I order two bagels, scrambled eggs with bacon and hash browns on the side, and coffee. When I finish, I eat a strawberry cheese Danish. Then Matt arrives, and we greet each other warmly.

Although we're very different, we're very close. Matt is my youngest sibling and the only one living at home. Our parents treated all of us as adults from an early age, so we experienced little sibling rivalry. My sisters are twins, and they, too, have always gotten along great. They're in college in California. Matt tells me that our parents, who are employed by the City of Commack, are still at work. He wants us to meet Mom and Dad at noon for lunch.

"I'll try," I tell him, "but I have a summer job, so I have to get back to the City."

When we enter my uncle's room, he can hardly open his eyes. He's on a ventilator. He recognizes me and motions for Matt to wait outside.

My uncle removes the breathing tube and makes an effort to speak. "I know I only have a few weeks to live." His voice is weak and raspy. I lean closer to understand him. "I want you to know that I have left all my inheritance to you. If you wish, you can distribute the money among your brother and sisters, or you may do whatever you like. I love all of you, but you are the wisest. And you're the one who treated me like a second father."

I continue talking with him until the nurse comes in and forces him to put on the oxygen again. I give him a long hug and leave.

"What did he tell you?" Matt asks. He has been waiting outside the door. I decide to keep it to myself.

"I'll tell you later. I'd rather not talk about it now."

We go on to meet my parents at their workplace. They're busy, so we all hug, and I promise to come home for a weekend. Matt takes me to the train station where I catch the 11 a.m. train.

CHAPTER 33

WEEK TWO

When I return to Manhattan, I go straight to the office. Mr. Petro is in a meeting with two newspaper directors, and Esperanza is with them. I decide to drink the cortadito that I have just purchased. Then I go downstairs to grab some lunch.

My WhatsApp indicates a message has just arrived. It's Esperanza. She must have seen me come in. She says that Mr. Petro wants to have lunch with me.

Since I have to wait for him, I attempt to befriend one of the men in the editing department. He's checking on news coming in from Iraq. I sit next to him. Everyone knows me by now since I've caused a lot of commotion in the past few days. They've never met a summer job trainee like me, one who has caused so much talk. They consider me tumultuous.

The fellow in the editing department is also of Latin background. He's friendly and says his name is Pedro. "Esperanza really digs you," he says and grins. "She talks about you and the group you have formed all the time. She says you are the new newspeople."

"Esperanza exaggerates."

"Really, she thinks you have an incredible future in this business. Just make sure you don't do something new in my department and get me fired. Ja, ja!"

"Don't worry, Pedro. Please explain what you do here."

"Well, I prepare the final wording of all our editorials, and I review all the news. I polish and refine the contents. They call us editors the gatekeepers between the writer and the reader. We need to balance the content so that both parties are happy."

"So, Pedro, when my group finishes and documents all our findings, do I give the manuscript to your department for polishing?"

"Yes. We review everything before it's published. We need to ensure that the data is accurate. We get hundreds of letters a week complaining about errors. Some are actual, some are invented by troublemakers. I ensure that we have a backup for all our original stories. Yours is going to be the original of the year. That's why they approved a $25,000 expense account for you. Your story will be a Sunday paper feature. Your findings will be sold and shared with thousands of newswires and electronic services all over the world. This means your story will be translated into every language."

"If I decide to write a book on my subject, Pedro, will you edit it?"

"You name's Mitch, right?" I nod. "I've done a few

private editing jobs in the past," he continues. "They're time-consuming, but money talks. If there's good money in it for me, I'll do it. Why not?"

"I've just made a new responsible acquaintance, and I know you're going to be good with my manuscript." We shake hands.

Esperanza buzzes me to meet Mr. Petro and her at Good Stuff Diner. I arrive after a few minutes' walk. The diner is small, but the savory smell opens my appetite. Mr. Petro and Esperanza are waiting to order.

Mr. Petro looks up from his menu as I join them. "Mitch, let Esperanza order for you so we can talk."

"Okay."

Mr. Petro goes right to the heart of what he has to say. "Mitch, I like you. I like the way you operate. Today I met with two of my newspaper owners, and they gave me some inside information on a possible takeover from one of the biggest concerns in the industry. They want me to form a group of talented young men in the business, and after only one week of what I've seen and from what Esperanza tells me, I've included you in the possible deal. If the deal goes through, you'll have a permanent job, and I'll be giving you freelance possibilities. You'll need to form a group to work with you." He snaps his fingers. "One second! I just had an idea. You should form a company, and I'll make sure the new owners hire you for all their important investigative stories. There might be a lot of money in this."

Esperanza's eyes gleam with anticipation as I thank Mr.

Petro for his offer. "You're very kind. You haven't even seen my work."

"I've been in this business many years, and I can detect a first class professional when I see one."

Esperanza has ordered me a delicious looking, incredibly big, extra-thick juicy double hamburger with onions and bacon that I will not forget, along with a side of fries. I wash everything down with a milkshake. I must have gained a couple of pounds already. I've never eaten so much in my life. I leave the diner happy, full, and full of ideas.

What is happening to me? Am I just in the right place at the right time? Or is my personal performance causing all this serendipity that I call luck? I hope it's not dumb luck, but rather the result of extreme skill. As I once read, "Luck is when skill and opportunity come together."

This job may be my opportunity to jump-start my future. I want to do so many things. Should I start now? I need to find someone to whom I can delegate my responsibilities. I'm on a positive streak, but I can't devote all ten weeks to this project. I need to empower someone with overseeing parts of the project that I supervise. All my team is busy—except maybe for Shirley. She said that she is just in NYC to practice piano at Juilliard, and in three months she starts her classes. Maybe I'll talk to her.

CHAPTER 34

ESPERANZA'S THOUGHTS

'm thirty-six years old. When I was eighteen, I followed a man to the United States because he said he was in love with me. I married him, but soon I realized that I was only one of his many loves. By then, I was a US citizen and in my third year of college. I decided to stay in this land of opportunity.

Little by little, I was able to legally bring members of my family to New York. I never re-married, although not for lack of proposals. I got this job when the newspaper opened ten years ago. I'm the administrative secretary for Mr. Petro.

Mr. Petro runs the newspaper. At first, he was just another boss, but as time went by, I noticed that he was what my Jewish friends call a *mensch*, someone to admire, someone noble, a human being to emulate. He's kind to everyone.

Little by little, I discovered that Mr. Petro's private life is miserable. His wife makes his life intolerable. She doesn't stop making his life impossible for a moment.

One day while she was berating him over the phone, he left his receiver open on his desk and went to the men's room. I noticed that he'd left his phone off the hook, so I went into his office to replace the receiver. His wife, unaware that he had laid down the phone, continued to insult him, give him orders, and offend him nonstop. I rushed out of his office—but not before Mr. Petro saw me. I feared for my job and expected to be fired. But I underestimated this kind man. Since I've been here, he has never fired anyone.

One day he came to work embittered. I could not stop myself. I followed him into his office and closed the door. I was crying silently, feeling his misery, and I wanted to calm him. Without a word I hugged him. I didn't want to let him go. He stayed still, and I cried silently with him. I have never felt such a moving experience. At that moment, we fell in love.

After years of torture, instead of getting divorced or going for couples counseling or psychological help, Mr. Petro hired a private detective to follow her. That's how he discovered her affair with a married man. Mr. Petro was never unfaithful to his wife until last week, when she left the house with all her belongings.

That day was the first time we were together. He feels that now is the time to re-do his life. Today he told me that he never had a child, and that he wants to marry me and make me pregnant. This man Mitch—his presence has changed my life.

CHAPTER 35

DR. SCOTT'S HOPES

itch has been my best friend since I was seven. I'm two years older than he is, but he was mature at a younger age than most kids. I think he was mature because of the way his parents brought them up. From the beginning the children had duties and obligations. They had to be neat, punctual, and get excellent grades. They had to earn the right to go to the movies or to a game. Whatever they did, they earned the right to do it.

I became friendly with him because he's extremely bright. I wanted to hang out with a bright friend because my father said that intelligence rubs off on people who hang out with intelligent people.

Mitch and I played together and went to the movies together. When we started to play chess, I would beat him easily, but not for long. He reached a level where neither I nor my father, his father, or uncle could win one game. As a freshman, he became our high school champion.

I finished medical school and we never lost contact. Mitch is a buddy for life.

I've been so busy with my residency and medical school that I've feared getting involved in a relationship. Many girls in school, nurses galore, and even some patients, have shown interest in me, but I can't be dishonest and tie up a girl at this stage of my life. I don't have time to dedicate to someone if I fall in love.

How many stories have I heard about so and so who got married, but the marriage didn't last because there was no time, no patience. A friend recently told me, "I helped him finish medical school, I took care of our children, I cooked, I did everything for him, and now that he's established, he leaves me for an eighteen year old.

This is not going to happen to me—or so I think. But when I met Kathy at the newspaper reunion and then at the picnic, something strange began to happen. I can't stop thinking about her. I've been bewitched. What the hell is happening to me?

CHAPTER 36

THE DAY CONTINUES

What a day! It seems as if all these days are days to remember. Now I have another job offer, and this one seems huge—full of responsibilities. I take a bus toward Central Park and take time off from my ever-changing thought pattern. Everyday something new occurs.

I check my WhatsApp; it's loaded with information. Everyone is interconnected and doing his job. Maybe I don't need to delegate; performing has become automatic. Everyone is conscientious about doing his part to make this experiment successful.

After reviewing the opportunity that Mr. Petro mentioned to me, I'm making a team for my future company. I immediately think of Mr. Bayley. He's a man on the go who recognizes talent when he sees it. I had this same feeling about him during college, and he maintains that same attitude now. I must consult with him. He would be the ideal person to manage my future company.

I don't know what prompts me, but I go back to my Craigslist e-mail and start searching for someone who's into investigation and who's looking for a temporary apartment. After going through many CVs, I find two persons in these categories and decide to invite them to the bookstore tomorrow morning, one at ten and the other at eleven.

Shirley called while I was at lunch, so I call her back now. She wants to see me about something. She can't talk at the moment. I tell her that I'll meet her at Starbucks at five.

When I hang up, Leslie calls to ask about my trip to see my uncle. I tell her that he's very ill, and that I'll explain later. She seems interested in being alone with me, and what that means, I need to figure out.

When I stop short of my subway station to buy a couple of hot dogs from a street vendor, I start to feel a little dizzy. I have not been able to go to the bathroom since yesterday, and I think I'd better call Scott. I used to be so regular.

Scott tells me that he has to speak with me privately because he has a major problem brewing.

"Okay," I say, "Tonight at eight, my apartment." At six, I am to meet Leslie, and at five, Shirley. Too many personal problems to resolve in person, I'm thinking. Esperanza texts, asking me to meet her at a coffee shop near work at seven tomorrow morning. My schedule is becoming complicated. Scott calls back after reading about constipation and tells me to drink a lot of water and take two teaspoons of Metamucil in a big glass of water before going to sleep tonight. Just before I arrive at Starbucks, Kathy calls. She, too, needs to speak with me privately. My God, what's happening? A few moments ago, I thought everything was on automatic pilot.

Shirley is waiting. I tell Kathy that I will go by her office at nine tomorrow. I think I need to go to the bathroom. Starbuck's bathrooms are usually clean. I hurry into the men's room. It's good that I haven't bought the Metamucil. I don't need it anymore. What a relief! Fat people must have this I-just-lost-a-hundred-pounds feeling after using the bathroom.

Shirley asks me to follow her to her apartment, so I do. "I need to be alone with you to explain," she says. "I know you're not stupid." She speaks with such seriousness that I have to follow her play. When we close the door, she hugs me with real sensuality and tenderness. I hug her back.

After a few minutes she says, "Thank you, Mitch. I really needed to hug you. I know what you're thinking." She leads me to the sofa and we sit. "You think I feel that I'm in love with your personality, with your leadership, with your eyes— with all of you. And I am—but it's a feeling that I know is not real, even though I wish it were. I hope that someday I find and fall in real love with someone like you, and that he falls in love with the real me. I'm a decisive person. I want you to know that I volunteered because I wanted to be near you. Now I realize that you're the one who initiated my return to normalcy. I will lower my weight substantially, and keep it off—but for me, not you. I'll be your most ardent volunteer. Trust me, I won't play around with my emotions. I'm a realist."

I kiss her softly and hug her. We stay like this for a while. Then I tell her, "If you think that I feel differently toward you because you're overweight, if you think I don't have positive feelings toward you, if you think that similar thoughts didn't go through my mind, you're wrong. My admiration for your uniqueness is extraordinary." She continues to shed tears, and we decide to go back to Starbucks.

It's almost six. George has arrived with Kim and Leslie. I excuse myself and go out for a talk with Leslie. She's agitated. "What's happened?" I ask.

"It's just that this summer job is so stupid. I have to get them to change my duties. I'm the coffee girl and the delivery girl." I understand her dilemma and nod. "I'm really obeying Kathy and Scott's food program, and I feel good about this," she continues. "And I'm helping Kim and George with all the food preparation."

"Leslie," I say, "study the project they're into and draw up an alternate plan to their design for an important portion of the project. Give it to the project manager's secretary, and wait and see what happens. Make sure to make friends with the key employees, especially the secretaries. They always know what's going on. It's too bad there are no male secretaries, because if you dressed a bit sexier, you could win anyone over. You're a hot summer intern."

Leslie likes that observation. "Okay, Mitch, I'll follow your advice. I hope you take what I'm about to say the right way, and I never ever thought I would say what I'm about to say."

"Go ahead. Say it, already."

She stares straight into my eyes and speaks slowly. "If you desire me, I'm yours. Right now, tomorrow, whenever. For a few minutes, for a day, and without any complications. You turn me on, like, incredibly."

I blush. Then I grab her hand and we go to my apartment. Once inside, I hug her and kiss her lightly. "There's a time and place for everything, and now is not the right time or the right place. Yes, I would love to be with you, but I'm not going to take a chance on jeopardizing our plan. You're definitely special to me." With that we return to Starbucks, holding hands.

The group chats, and then I tell them that I have a doctor's appointment at eight that evening and cannot continue with today's planned exercise. After the meeting, I decide to go back to my apartment to wait for Scott, who arrives at 8:15 p.m.

Scott's expression looks strange. Something has happened to my friend. "So, what's going on?"

"It's all your fault."

"What's my fault?"

"Why the hell did you have to bring me into your experiment?"

This is not the Scott I know. I've never seen him this agitated. "What's wrong? Did you get in trouble at the hospital?"

"No! It's this woman that you assigned me to work with on your plan's diet. Kathy! She's the problem."

I can't imagine Kathy being difficult to work with. "Why? What did she do?"

Scott begins pacing and shaking his head. "Nothing, nothing. Nothing at all." He stops and faces me. "I have simply fallen totally in love with her."

I repress my laughter and ask, "Does she feel the same?"

"I don't know. Maybe?" Scott resumes pacing. "She has totally destabilized me. I can't work, I can't sleep, my appetite has disappeared. Man, this is crazy!"

"Well, tell her."

"How? I've never felt like this before. You know that. Of all the girls I've dated, many were one-night stands so I had no special emotion, no special feelings. Just *wham, bam, thank you, ma'am.* That was it. With Kathy, I haven't even dated her. All I've done is spoken with her to plan meals. I'm going crazy over her. Dear friend, I came here for help."

He's really in bad shape. "Do you want me to call her? She must be out in the park with the group."

"No, please don't get involved. She's a dream come true, and I can't afford to lose her. If you get involved, she's going to choose you. All the women we meet want you. I'm not exaggerating."

"Stop saying things that aren't true. You're handsome *and* you're a physician. Women go crazy over doctors." I have two beers left over from the other day, so we drink and relax. Scott thanks me for my free psychotherapy session.

"I feel much better. I'm going to the park now, and I'll let you know if I survive."

NEXT DAY FULL OF EVENTS

Alexa didn't awaken me. I check her out. Marcello probably unplugged her last night so he could iron his shirt. "Marcello, wake up. It's 6 a.m. Don't you have a video conference with someone? And please, next time don't unplug Alexa. Thank you."

I arrive at Union Square at exactly 7 a.m. There she is, that good-looking lady with that beautiful smile in place. This time, Esperanza invites me for a cortadito.

"Do you still have relatives in Venezuela?" I ask.

"Of course. All Venezuelans are my relatives."

"Too bad that country has such extreme political problems."

She nods and sips her cortadito. "How is the plan going?"

"All is well." She orders a big breakfast for both of us, and then tells me why she wanted to meet me. "Mitch, is your last name Jewish?"

"No, why?"

"I thought you were Jewish."

"Well, I am. My mother is Jewish and my father isn't. In the Jewish religion, the mother's womb is what makes you Jewish."

"So do you practice Judaism?"

"Yes. I was bar mitzvahed at thirteen. I fast on Yom Kippur, and sometimes I go to synagogue. On Passover, I eat matzah instead of bread. Why do you ask?"

"Would you marry a non-Jewish woman?"

"I don't know. I haven't thought about the Jewish implications."

"Well, don't worry. I'm not trying to get my Graciela married to a Jewish man yet. By the way, she'll be back soon. I really want you to meet her—but just as a friend, understand? No monkey business, *entendido?*"

I smile.

"Look friend," she continues, "this is confidential. Pedro and I think he's getting a divorce soon. Yesterday, he asked me to marry him. He is the greatest guy in the world. I know that he's Jewish, so I'm sure his family won't be happy with me. He hasn't even touched the subject. But I want to convert as soon as possible. I'll do anything for that man. I love him deeply and with such sincerity that I can't even explain it to you. Can you put me in contact with a rabbi? Perry has suffered so much with his failed marriage. You can't imagine how terrible a life he's had."

I understood the situation. "Find out if his family is Orthodox, Conservative, or Reform, because each has a different type of synagogue. We need to get the right rabbi."

"Okay, I'll find out. He goes to one—wait. The address is 650 something on Lexington Ave."

"I'll Google it . . . Okay, it's a Reform synagogue, which will probably be easier. But Israel won't accept the conversion. Israel requires an Orthodox conversion, which is more difficult. You're lucky you're not a man, so you won't have to be circumcised."

"Wow! I am lucky!"

"Good luck, my friend. Now let's go to work."

When I sign in, Pedro gives me a smile. Now I have a new friend in Pedro. I bring him a cortadito and he says *chevere*. I google *chevere*. It's Spanish for cool.

I rush to my next appointment, this one with Kathy. I check the WhatsApp, and all is going well. I put in my data for breakfast. I'm happy.

Kathy is attending a paying customer, so I wait.

"I made super-fat brownies especially for you," Kathy says, offering me a brownie that I can't refuse. I love brownies. That's funny; she's in a super-duper mood. Or is she using reverse psychology on me? I don't know. But so many things are happening that I can't wait to start my book chronicling the project. I'm accumulating so much material.

"I called you yesterday, Mitch," Kathy begins, "because I had a dramatic personal problem, but last night it was resolved. That's why I made you super-special brownies."

"Oh, great. Are you going to share what happened, or is it private?"

"Actually, you should have guessed. Your dear best friend

Scott has been behaving totally abnormally for a grown, educated, medical practitioner—and one with certain stature, I might add. Last night, while I was finishing the exercise classes that I am supposed to give to our group, Scott came up to me and in front of everyone, grabbed me and kissed me forcefully. I responded with equal fervor, and everyone applauded. It's no secret any more. We're madly in love.

"I called my parents this morning—they live in New Zealand. They told me to ask him, to marry me. That's the way my family does things. He's asked me out on our first date tonight, so I'm going to ask him to marry me right off. Don't worry; it will take a few weeks. My parents will need time to sail here since they want to be present for the ceremony. My mom is afraid of flying, so they'll travel by ship."

I hug her and congratulate her. "I'm sure Scott will make you happy. He's Irish, and they love to be merry."

My God! I hurry to The Strand bookstore. I don't even pause to check my mail for appointment confirmations. I don't like to be late for appointments.

CHAPTER 38

MY NEW IDEA

A t ten I am to meet Tommy, an MIT engineering graduate. I have to tell him that I don't have a room for him anymore. I forgot to put on my green shirt, so I decide to write *Tommy* on a sheet of paper and see if he sees it.

A bald guy comes up and asks, "What color shirt were you supposed to wear?"

"Green." He shakes my hand in relief.

"Finally, I will have somewhere to sleep."

"Listen, let's go to the corner for a coffee."

"Why don't we go to the apartment? I have my bag near the cashier."

"Tommy, wait a minute. I have to explain something."

"What? Don't tell me this is a fake advertisement? Please don't tell me that."

"One second, Tommy. I need to make a phone call." I move over to another bookshelf for privacy. "Esperanza, I need a big favor."

"Yes. Ask."

"I need to place someone in your house for nine weeks."

"What? Are you crazy?"

"I'll explain later."

"Well, okay. You must have a good reason. Bye."

I rejoin Tommy who looks distressed. "It's okay, Tommy. I have a room for you, but it's not in my apartment. It's at a friend's house. Now let's sit down and have a coffee." I explain my experiment and all about my team as fast as I can. He's not an easy type, and he has a sense of distrust. He must have had bad experiences in the past.

"I'm here for a short review of a government contract in the area of high tech," Tommy says. "I'm doing this for peanuts, but I expect an incredible job offer after this project is approved. Right now, I'm short on money because I just got divorced, and my ex got everything.

"Please wait for me. I have another appointment, but it will only take a moment." I leave with a new sheet of paper on which I've printed *Paul*. At eleven sharp, I stand waiting with my sign. Beside me is a young woman who keeps looking at her watch.

"You seem annoyed by people who don't keep their appointments," I say. "I feel the same way."

"I'm supposed to be waiting for a man in a green shirt."

"Are you—Paula?" She nods. "Oops, I'm sorry. I thought you were a man. And I forgot to put on my green shirt."

Her mood changes. "No worries," she says, relieved. "I'm glad we found each other."

"I have another person waiting to be interviewed in a coffee shop nearby. Would you mind if I interviewed both of you together?"

"One second. You offered me a room, not an interview."

"Let me explain. I—"

"Are you a Craigscammer?" she interrupts. "I'm going to call 911!"

"Please don't. Here's my ID. I work for *The Daily Flash*. I'm an honest person, really." I press my ID into her hand. "Keep my ID until you hear me out. Keep my wallet, too. I'm not trying to cheat or steal or anything." She calms down and agrees to go to the coffee shop.

I introduce her to Tommy and order her a coffee. They chat while I call Scott. I tell him that I need his extra bed for a while, and he doesn't ask why or for whom. He is in the happiest of moods, and he doesn't even know that tonight, he's going to get engaged.

My two new recruits are tired and hungry. "I know a place with fabulous hamburgers," I say, and they accept. After seeing my eyes, Paula returns my ID and wallet. She hands Tommy his credentials. We walk a half a block to the restaurant where I order the same hamburger I had yesterday. One must be over 7000 calories, but I love it.

I explain everything. Both are average, non-techie people, so it isn't easy to explain that I need someone with the ability to make a sophisticated app—an app that I can present to both Apple and Microsoft for weight control. I read in their CVs that they each have vast experience in this area.

Paula is more relaxed after the meal and understands my challenge. I promise to compensate them economically as soon as I can sell or implement the app. I am vague, of course. I have no idea what to offer them. It's a wild guess that the app will be a success. Only then will I share the profits with them.

To my surprise, both accept. They have to hang out with me, so they join me for my 5 p.m. meeting at Starbucks where everything will become clear. Paula will go to Esperanza's house, and Tommy to Scott's. What a day!

By 6 p.m. everyone has arrived. Mr. Petro comes with Esperanza. I greet him and in a low voice say *mazel tov*. He winks his approval. I am lucky that Starbucks is not too busy at this hour, so I am able to introduce everyone and welcome them to our team. Esperanza cannot wait for me to learn about the sudden roommate she has acquired, so I explain. Marcello films the gathering non-stop. Scott and Kathy are hand in hand, and I have a good feeling about my whole group. I love each of them, even the newcomers. They all make me feel accomplished.

CHAPTER 39

THE NEWCOMERS

I sit down to look at Paula's CV. Now I remember that she has a degree in computer science from Berkeley, a post-graduate mention in robotics from Stanford, and she has been involved in special assignments for Microsoft, Google, and now Amazon. Why does a person with such qualifications need to stay in a temporary room? She should have sufficient funds to stay in a hotel—or to rent a furnished loft in Manhattan.

She has expressed a lack of confidence in me from the beginning, and yet she still continues within the group. She might be seriously weird. I need to pay special attention to her activities and volunteerism. I ask her what her job is in Manhattan.

"Oh, I needed some time off, so I came to the city to hang out for a few weeks."

Distrust seems to be her motto. I need to be sure that I've chosen a reliable person for my new idea of incorporating an app in conjunction with our experiment. I also need to be able to count on the person for our final-result document to be published in *The Daily Flash* and in my forthcoming book, *Body Shapers Dream Team*. My book, if catalogued as the new achievement of the moment, will generate news and commentaries worldwide.

I decide to invite Paula for a private breakfast near the newspaper. Paula is sleeping at Esperanza's, so I'll ask Esperanza to bring her to work with her in the morning to show her our work installations. I'll ask Esperanza to be as friendly as possible toward Paula and to find out as much as she can about her. I need to know whether to stay with her or ask her to leave our group.

In contrast, Tommy integrated with the group immediately. He has become everyone's friend and is full of positive advice in every aspect of all the conversations. He seems interested in Esperanza, because every time Mr. Petro moves away from her, he tries to take his place. I had to tell him that she is engaged to my boss.

I make an appointment with Tommy for 9 a.m. at the newspaper office. He tells me he has time, and that most of his work is done online anywhere. He mentions that he needed to get away after the very difficult divorce he went through in Boston, and that New York was a place to get lost and maybe enjoy himself. He also mentions that his luck has changed in that he has just met a great group with whom to work.

I'm ready to go. I follow Shirley and Leslie to their apartment, hug them both, and go home to sleep after a very hectic day.

CHAPTER 40

WEEK TWO AND A HALF

Alexa does her job. I shower, eat a protein bar and a large banana, and rush to get to the office on time. Marcello follows me. He's enthusiastic over the video footage he has accumulated and mentions that he may make a film from the content. His main summer job is sporadic, so he has lots of free time. He also enjoys the group's company, especially Leslie's—or so I think.

Scott awakened me at 2 a.m. to tell me that he had just been proposed to, and Tommy was his witness. I shook my head. *I had some meshuggeneh volunteers here.*

Paula and Esperanza are at the coffee shop and seem to have connected because they're both very happy about something. Paula gets up and, with a smile that's worth a million bucks, asks me for a hug. I accede to her wish or demand. It seems that Esperanza has done her job of neutralizing Paula's insecurity or distrust.

We go up to the office and show Paula around. I introduce

her to Pedro and the others. Mr. Petro shows her a space where she can work that she can Tommy can share. "I'm allotting you this space as a favor to Mitch. The app project has nothing to do with the paper. We're just collaborating with Mitch."

Paula and I go down to the diner for breakfast. Tommy appears ahead of time. I don't care, since I feel that Paula's distrust has been neutralized. I have both newcomers talk with each other and discuss what they are going to need to implement the app. They decide to make two apps, one for the overweight and one for the underweight.

We enjoy a hearty breakfast during which they discuss their professional achievements and goals. These two are going to do a superb job. They speak the same technical language, and they understand one another. I predict that they will be successful. I give them the option to be present at all our meetings and workouts. When I want to touch on the fee, both answer simultaneously that there will be time for that later.

"We're volunteers who want to help. Thank you, Mitch, for choosing us. It seems we both need this job. No pressure, no deadlines—we have good vibes."

They leave for their new office to begin planning.

CHAPTER 41

CALL TO MR. BAYLEY

I double check our group's WhatsApp and put in all my pertinent information. Everything is running smoothly. The underweight and the overweight pairs have reported that their goals are fine-tuned. This news couldn't be better. Their motivation is a factor that cannot be duplicated in real life. The pairs each have a large group to whom they respond, and many people are rooting for their well-being. Those in charge of food purchase, production, and delivery have performed an A+ job. Everything has gone without a hitch.

I head to the mid-Manhattan public library with no specific goal in mind. I want to research the science of weight loss more deeply. In my first look at the results of the biggest loser, a well-known research scientist with the National Institute of Health (NIH) saw participants losing twenty pounds a week. However, their diets were severely restrictive and the workouts punishing. The results of his findings were that thirteen of the fourteen contestants gained an average of 66% of their weight back.

This data is depressing. People who read this will immediately think *Why should I bother if I'll gain all the lost weight back?* This study prompted the NIH to invest even more money into the problem. They concluded that each diet has to be personalized to be effective. In most studies where the data is positive, no two people lost weight in the same way. One ate less caloric foods, others exercised more. I want to see what our mini experiment concludes.

I call my instructor, Mr. Bayley, and ask him several questions to determine his availability for a possible company that I will need to organize if a deal comes through. He says that a meeting between us will determine his interest. We make an appointment for the next day for lunch at a Midtown restaurant. I have to be clear on what I am going to propose to him. I need to discuss this with someone who knows about this subject, so I call Mr. Petro—who else?

Scott calls and asks if I want to have lunch with him and says that this time, he's not going to stand me up. I agree and meet him at 12:30, but he isn't alone. Kathy is with him. They're both beaming with million-dollar smiles. They reiterate their wows and tell me their future plans. Scott wants me to be his best man.

I ask how they determined the ideal diet for the four participants. Kathy tells me that she majored in nutrition before pursuing her post-graduate studies in psychology. She shows me a paper she happens to have prepared as an example of what she will advise the overweight to do after our experiment is concluded:

Breakfast: mixed vegetable omelet, Greek yogurt parfait, burritos

Mid-morning snack: fresh fruit, hard-boiled egg, nuts, and assorted vegetables

Lunch: turkey avocado wraps, chili with corn bread, organic soups, salads

Mid-afternoon snack: homemade granola nut bars, fresh hummus, assorted vegetables, nuts

Dinner: mahi-mahi with steamed vegetables, Hawaiian chicken bowl, chicken cacciatore

I am impressed by her organized approach, but at first glance, I think it's an excessive amount of food.

"I recommend weighing the food," she says, "because the portions have to be small. Most foods are low in calories but high in fiber to help you feel full longer. By eating five or six small meals and snacks a day, you keep your sugars and hunger under control. I also recommend avoiding caffeine and drinking six to eight glasses of water a day."

I look down on the paper she gave me to see what she recommends for the underweight:

Eat more frequently: Underweight persons feel full faster so they need to eat five or six full meals during the day instead of the three regular meals.

Choose food rich in nutrients: Eat lots of nuts and seeds, pastas and cereals, whole grain breads.

Make every bite count: Eat cheese, nuts, avocados and dried fruits. Make wraps with lean meats and spreads.

Make sure of what you drink: If you fill up by drinking fluids, don't drink low-calorie drinks. They will stop you from eating. Drink high-calorie drinks at least a half an hour after your meal

Add Extras: After you prepare your meal, add extras like lean meats, cheeses, nuts, or seeds. An occasional scrambled egg is also advised.

Take an additional treat: You can always use an extra granola bar or a slice of your favorite vanilla ice cream bar. Keep in mind to avoid excess sugar and fat. Instead have a bran muffin, a yogurt, and some berries.

Exercise—the best is strength training: Exercise builds up your muscles and will help you gain weight besides stimulating your appetite.

This conversation makes me happy. I have acquired simple solutions for many people's complex problems.

I return to *The Daily Flash* and wait for Mr. Petro to receive me. He invites me for a coffee. Since lunch wasn't very filling, I order a large pizza with all the toppings, and he joins me for a slice.

"It's best to start organizing the paperwork for the State

of New York. That way, when the deal goes through, you won't lose valuable time because you'll be ready to take on the contract that I will offer."

"So, what exactly are we going to be doing?"

"I'll give you a list of topics that your team will use for investigative reporting. These topics will provide a constant flow of stories that my new company will be able to sell to other news corporations. Your team will investigate and corroborate the veracity of the stories. Besides reporters, you'll need videographers, photographers, and narrators. We'll pay your company for all the services rendered to us, and, if you're really good, maybe you can attract other clients like FOX, CNN, and other networks here and abroad."

"Mr. Petro, this operation sounds big."

"Yes, it can be—if you make it big."

"Will I need to invest? From what you tell me I'm going to need a big office and an organization."

"Yes, you probably will. I'm assuming that this deal goes through."

"What are the chances?"

"Today I was told that it was a done deal. In two weeks we should close."

"Are you going to stay on with the new company?"

"They offered me the presidency."

"Wow, congratulations are in order."

"Wait. Let them make it official."

I leave his office mesmerized. I cannot believe what Mr. Petro has offered me. I have to think and plan. Where am I going to get money for such a big project? I'll have to consult. I'll sleep on it and see what comes up.

That afternoon we meet as usual at Starbucks. The manager is really cool. He has one of his employees set up the tables and reserve them for my group at 6 p.m. every weekday. We meet, talk, have coffee, and then go to Central Park for our routine exercise.

CHAPTER 42

SOON, THE END OF WEEK TWO

After the exercise session, I ask the group to weigh themselves and send the data. Kim expects to give us a preliminary rundown of all the data accumulated to date, but he needs the exact information from the starting point of the experiment.

Paula and Tommy ask to meet with me, but my two girls, Shirley and Leslie, expect me to hang out with them. I tell the girls to eat their prepared meals and that they can accompany me for my dinner after I meet with the scientists—the new name that Paula and Tommy have acquired.

Paula has evidently taken over the leadership of their project. Tommy has become visibly submissive. Once again, I envision something developing between them—but this notion may be just a feeling or wish. Tommy needs affection, and I don't know if Paula is the type to supply his needs.

They explain their progress and conclude saying, "May we have some money to buy the special technical gadgets?"

"How much do you need?"

"A couple thousand." They detect my hesitancy and assume I cannot supply. "No problem," Paula says. "I'll put up the money."

"Thank you. I promise to reimburse everything as soon as I have the funds." They invite me to a fancy five-star restaurant, but I decline because not only can I not afford it but the girls are waiting. I hear that they invited and went with Mr. Petro and Esperanza.

Later Esperanza tells me that Paula is wealthy, that she hates to stay alone in hotels, and that she's a very lonely woman. This is why she resorted to Craigslist to find a roommate.

My two girls and I go to Whole Foods where I overstuff myself with a little of everything. I already have difficulty closing my pants, and I need a new hole punched in my belt. The girls' affection for me is no secret. Even Marcello has become a bit jealous. I tell him to find company, that he no doubt has the ability. George and Kim are always busy with the food. Shirley makes plans for a weekend outing on Staten Island, and I want to go to sleep. I'm pooped.

Lately my good sound sleep is being interrupted by a new kind of stress, one that I haven't experienced before. I beat Alexa's wake-up call by two hours today. In a way, this is good because I have more time to think and plan in the quiet of the dawn. I make my daily to-do list, putting *call Matt* at the top of the list. I want to ask my brother how our uncle is doing. Then I want to get together with Scott's Uncle Marvin who said he has interesting things to tell me regarding my area of interest. I have to stop by our office and meet with Mr. Bayley. If I have time, I would also like to meet with a man who says hypnosis worked for him in weight loss.

Marcello gets up early and tells me he has a job interview at a different network. He does not enjoy what he's doing in his regular summer job. He also mentions that he has met a woman who has undergone bariatric surgery whom he thinks I may want to meet.

I leave the house early and go to a Greek diner for a super-special early bird $4.99 all-you-can-eat breakfast. The catch is that they start you off with great coffee and a large strawberry Danish, limiting your consumption because you're full already.

A young woman is sitting right in front of me, and she, too, has come for the special. When I see her face, I notice that her eyes are extraordinarily beautiful. They're eye-catching, impossible to avoid. When she sees me looking at her that way, she sees my incredible eyes. We are locked in a staring contest. We both laugh simultaneously, which, of course, leads to our introducing ourselves. Natalia is around twenty-five, as tall as I am, blonde, and she wears different earrings on each ear and an array of rings on several fingers. We chat, and she accepts an invitation for coffee at my usual Starbucks for this evening. I am concerned that someone has attracted me so much. I have enough girls interested in me; why did I invite this one? Why am I trying to start a relationship with a complete stranger?

Her eyes, her personality, her magnetism—something attracted me intensely, and I wanted to find out what.

Esperanza has not arrived, but I have a short conversation with Pedro. He asks if I've heard the buyout rumors. I hesitate before deciding that to pursue the topic is not going to contribute to something positive, so I don't answer.

Mr. Petro greets me and waves me in the direction of his office. He has a secretary bring us coffee and then closes his door. "Mitch, you've been such a positive addition to my life that I must confide in you. I know that Esperanza has spoken with you about our relationship, and everything she has told you is true. I have fallen in love with this unique woman. She is so different from me and from my environment. Just her presence makes me happy. Please forgive me. I need to speak with someone about what is happening to me. You're so dynamic that I feel you're the right listener right now." Tears form in his eyes. I get up and gave him a man-hug, which he appreciates. "Esperanza went to the synagogue that you suggested," he continues, "and she has already started conversion classes. I'm so happy. I had to share this with you."

I leave to meet Uncle Marvin who lives on First Ave and 23rd St. I walk as the day is marvelous.

Marvin is glad to see me. I have the feeling that he doesn't often receive visitors. His wife has prepared all kinds of sweets, and since I'm overdue for a snack, I eat. I make a mental note to buy a bigger belt and new pair of pants since these are too tight.

Marvin was a soccer coach in college, but following a

skiing accident, he's led a sedentary life. He devotes most of his life to helping children with physical handicaps. He knows that I'm interested in how he got so fat.

"My weight gain started after my skiing accident. I was bedridden for months. In those days, all I did was read, watch TV, and eat. My wife worked, and I was alone. The TV programs were boring. They didn't have Netflix or movies-on-demand like today, so I ate and ate myself to this. I've gone on many binge diets. I've attempted almost everything in the book, including fad diets, but in the end, I've abandoned every one of them. They caused me immense stress and suffering. I remember one diet from Switzerland where they assign a fat person a cow and promise that if drinks its milk for a week, he will lose a dramatic amount of weight. Most of these gimmicks don't work.

"I've even tried hypnosis. Hypnosis did help me shed a few extra pounds, but without a diet program, the weight loss didn't last. I received counseling, I added exercise—but there isn't enough scientific evidence about weight loss through hypnosis alone.

"Then I started with food supplements like *garcinia cambogia*, which is supposed to suppress my love for sweets. Probably the fruit is a psychosomatic tool that marketers use. I've tried pills that supposedly make people lose weight, and I've gone to camps that offer extreme weight-loss programs. All these approaches caused suffering, and disillusion was always the result." I thanked my new friend for his clear message: *To achieve success in dieting is very difficult.*

Next is Mr. Bayley's lunch appointment. I take a downtown bus and get off at Times Square. He has suggested *Bistango* at The Kimberly Hotel because he knows someone there, and the food is good. I asked if it's expensive, and he said that today I would be his guest.

I check it out and find that *Bistango* is an Italian, gluten-free restaurant. I then think that he may have celiac disease, but this is just a thought. He arrives in time and offers me an alcoholic beverage, something to which I'm unaccustomed. We students only drank cheap beer from the tap, $1 a drink. (The price went up on weekends.)

I have a whiskey on the rocks and he orders a martini. He wants me to give him a rundown on my project, which I do with pleasure.

"How about Rabbi Zwi's offer? Have you decided what you're going to tell him?"

"That was the first time anyone has offered me such an incredible job. I'm still surprised and keeping it as an incredible option."

"I see that you give diplomatic answers."

I wink at him as a way to inform him that I need more time. At the suggestion of the maître d', whom he apparently knows well, we both order the daily special—a seafood pasta. Then I launch into the reason for today's meeting.

"Mitch, call me Bayley. You're not my student anymore. We're equals; we're both journalists."

"Okay, Bayley. Suppose a big news network offers me the chance to establish an independent company that has all the personnel and know-how for investigative reporting. Furthermore, the company offers me an exclusive outsourcing contract. What would you say? What would you do? How would you organize it? How much financial support would you need to start up?"

Bayley is astounded by the immensity and complexity of my statements. "Is this a supposition or an actual offer?"

"It's a supposition, Bayley, but I need an answer as if it were an actual offer. What participation would I have in this supposition? I don't know yet, but I may need a managing director. Isn't that the way startups start?"

He remains pensive. "Now I know why you called me," he says slowly. "It's that article I wrote about this type of idea for a journalism magazine. Did you read the article?"

"I didn't."

"I'll send it to you. The article has the answers to your questions, except for the finances. We need to analyze the needs of the news network. I have a funny feeling that I know something about what you're insinuating, Mitch—rumors abound about buyouts and takeovers in our industry."

"Okay, I'll give you a ballpark figure: two million."

"You need to raise at least two million? I can probably get you some money from investors I know. If you're talking about a buyout that's rumored to occur, I'll put in some of my money, also. Do you have any money to invest?"

"My family might be interested. I don't know yet." We finish our meal, and I thank him for his time and invitation.

"Mitch, why do I have the feeling that you've just offered me a job?"

I smile. "Your intuition is excellent. I'll call you soon."

Wow, that interview was superb. I duck into the nearby public library and find his article. It's exactly what I need. What a stroke of luck!

I call my brother. He happens to be with our uncle at the hospital. "Here, Uncle, it's Mitch." He hands the receiver to my uncle.

"Hi, Mitch. I'm feeling better. They took out the oxygen tubes, and I can go home tomorrow."

"Oh, great news. I'll try to come down to see you and my parents."

"Why don't you come today?"

"I'm so absorbed with my job. Maybe tomorrow. I'm so happy that you're better." I hang up, pleased with the news.

The sky is beginning to cloud over. Rain is imminent. I run to the bus stop and head to my Starbucks. All I can think is what a day. What another incredible super day! What's going to happen next? Oh, yes I need a new pair of pants.

It's still early, so I'm alone at the Starbucks. I look back on the day. I've accomplished so many things, but one thing I don't understand. That girl Natalia—why do I want to see her again? She doesn't fit into my plan. She doesn't fit into my possible startup. She's pretty, and those eyes . . . But am I a man who falls for physical attributes? No! I look for intelligence, for a person with extraordinary abilities, for someone who can be useful in future projects.

What am I thinking? I suddenly feel my fast heart beat becoming faster. Am I having a tachycardia attack? I calm down when I see Shirley's now-familiar face. She comes up, gives me a kiss, and whispers pleasing sensual words in my ear: *You are my king. I can't stop thinking about you.*

This is all I need to hear to make me even more stressed. I get up and say, "I love you, too, but as a friend. I'm not at a place in my life where I can get emotionally involved. Please understand."

"Cool it," she says, smiling. "I'm kidding." She pauses, then adds, "But you'll be my best friend forever. You're the man who gave me back my life. I'm becoming a normal person because of you. I owe you."

"No—"

"My dieting has been incredible. I'm not hungry, and I'm not stressed—something that usually happens when I diet. I can't believe how stimulated I am to continue. When you see me in a few months you'll say, "Hey, babe! What a body, what a figure. Wow, you're my type of girl!""

"Shirley, you're an excellent composer and musician, and now I see you're an excellent actress as well." I applaud her monologue. We both laugh without control.

The friendly manager has witnessed the scene and also applauds her performance.

CHAPTER 43

PAULA'S THOUGHTS

I am Paula. I was under so much pressure at my Palo Alto company that I went to the airport and texted my people: *I'm getting lost for a few weeks.* I am going to Miami to have fun at the beach, get a suntan, and relax. Maybe I'll get lucky and pick up some Latino and have an affair.

I only imagine this since I know this is unlikely—not only because of my looks, but because this isn't me. I was describing the person I would like to be but who I'm not.

Enroute to the airport, the Uber driver told me, "I heard there's a warning for a possible hurricane in South Florida." This news made me change my itinerary. I approached the American Airlines ticket agent.

"When is your next flight to the East Coast?"

She checked her monitor. "Kennedy Airport in forty-five minutes."

"Okay, I'd like a seat."

"Looks like we're booked in economy. But I have one seat left in business."

"Okay, no problem." I handed her my American Express Black. She stared at the credit card as if to say, *This is yours? You don't look able to afford the card's annual $2500 fee.*

The Amex black is called the Centurion card. It's by invitation only to those who spend over $250,000 a year using their Amex card. So the Centurion card was given to me. The initiation fee was over $5000. All the members of my board of directors received it. I was the CEO of a new and fast-growing startup that was my idea, and in this hi-tech world, if you're lucky, you become rich fast. I was lucky.

Aboard the plane with no suitcase and only my briefcase and purse, it occurred to me to make a reservation at the Four Seasons. I tried, but they were booked. Out of curiosity, I searched on Craigslist and discovered an ad for a roommate. I attached my CV and changed my name on the first page from Paula to Paul. I figured the guy who placed the ad was looking for a male roommate. Maybe he was good looking. I was ready for an adventure.

When we landed in New York and I checked my phone, I was surprised to see that I had an 11 a.m. appointment with a Mitch at a bookstore that I love to visit. So I called an Uber. The rest you know.

This man Tommy—I really like him. He treats me like a goddess, and he doesn't even know me. I'm guessing he came to NY to recuperate from a tough divorce. I think he must be someone successful trying to look poor, just like me. I decide to join this group. I like Mitch; he is a fabulous young man with an incredible future. I'm even thinking of hiring him. No, I'm sure of it. The job will come with a $500K package. He's a very capable guy and a natural leader. I also love the idea of sitting down and creating an app like I did when I was at Stanford and Berkeley. I'm really enjoying this vacation. In fact, I feel like prolonging it. I feel like a kid again. The exercise is great, and the people in the group are all leaders. I want to do something for all of them—especially this Tommy who has such an incredible, caring, sweet personality. I can't get over him.

CHAPTER 44

STARBUCKS

By 6 p.m. most of my gang has arrived. I start by updating them on how well our plans are doing. I have
my back to the door, but when everyone leans to one
side to look, I turn to see what's distracting them. And that
is when I see that an angel has flown in. Since everyone is
looking at her, the only sound in Starbucks is silence.

"Hi, Natalia," I finally say. "Hey, everybody, this is
Natalia, a friend of mine." Leslie and Shirley stare at me—
no, everyone stares at me. They must be thinking *so this is
Mitch's secret.*

Kathy breaks the enchantment of the moment. "Hey
let's go. It's time to start our exercise. I want everyone to race
to our place in Central Park. The winner gets a free celery
stick." We all laugh and everyone but me takes off to the applause of the Starbucks staff.

"Come on, Natalia, join us," I say.

"I'm caught off guard. First of all, I didn't know about

your group, and if I'd known you were going to exercise, I wouldn't have worn these." She raised a leg to show her high heels. "In fact, I don't know anything about you."

"True, but I don't know anything about you, either."

"Fair enough. How about I meet you later? I need to change." She has a point. She's dressed like a high-grade executive who does business with the rich and mighty.

"We'll be at Central Park." I give her detailed directions to our exercise spot, and we part ways. I run back and catch up with her. "Can I have your number in case we got lost?"

"Give me yours, and I'll see if I want you to have mine." I give her my number, but she doesn't give me hers.

Natalia doesn't come to Central Park. She doesn't call me. I've lost her. That night, I don't join the group. I need some time to think things over. There comes a time in a person's life when he's on top of many happenings that need his attention, but when one doesn't work out, his life seems to stop, and he can't continue as before. That's how I feel at this moment at this hour. I lose myself in thought.

I go back to the Greek diner were I we met. She isn't there. Man, am I stupid. How could I expect her to be there? Insanity sometimes ensues in times like this. I eat a little but find I've lost my appetite.

I go straight to bed, but cannot fall asleep. Marcello comes in late. When he sees me awake and nervous, he offers me a sleeping pill from his first-aid kit. (I forgot to mention that he is a medicine and vitamin enthusiast.) He takes a pill for any reason from his collection of 100 pill bottles. I decide to take the sleeping pill. I need to rest. This woman is driving me crazy.

CHAPTER 45

THE SATURDAY

get up, and I'm a little groggy at first—part of the effects of the sleeping pill. I'd never taken one before. Alexa is the one who gets me up. If I hadn't asked her, I would have slept the whole day. My friend Marcello gave me a bomb pill.

I stop by the Greek diner again and have a bagel and coffee and then rush to catch the Long Island train to Commack. My brother can't pick me up, so I call an Uber and go straight to my parents' house. We talk, and I relate my activities and the plans and offers I've received.

"Well, good luck, Mitch. You're working hard, so you deserve all these opportunities." My father looks at me narrowly. "Do I detect stress in your voice and attitude?"

I decided not to tell them the cause is Natalia, about whom they don't even know. I brush off his comment. "Me stressed? Nonsense."

My uncle is pleased to see me. His face has the appearance of one who has been revived after a sure death. I hug him and tell him all my news. When I touch on the part about needing money for a project, he warns me that he will not touch his money. "Sorry, Mitch. I wish I could help you, but the doctor told me that now that I've survived this illness, I could live another twenty-five years. I just hope my savings last twenty-five years."

"I wish you well, Uncle. You'd better hang onto your savings, because you're going to live to be 120 like Moses. And don't worry about money, Uncle. I'll be around to make sure you live like a king."

I arrive back in Manhattan and communicate with the group. I need to return to overeating, so I head straight to the Greek diner again. I spot the same waiter who was there the day I met Natalia, and I ask if she's been back.

"No, she hasn't."

"Are you sure?"

"I'd have remembered her. She's special. No, that day you were here was the first and last time I saw her. She's not from around here," he adds.

"What makes you say that?"

"She looks rich. All that jewelry she wore was real; nothing was imitation. I worked in a jewelry store in Athens, and I know when something's real and when it's an imitation. She must live on Park Ave. At least, that's one of the places where only the wealthy live."

"Well, thanks anyway." The waiter started toward the kitchen and then turned back.

"You know, I'm sure I saw her picture in a magazine. Maybe she's a model?"

"When do you think you saw her picture?"

"Recently. Where was it? Let me think . . . Maybe in People magazine, or Sports Illustrated—I'm not sure."

My people are already enjoying themselves at the Blue Heron Park in Staten Island. I have created an incredible camaraderie among them. They are all volunteers; even Paula and Tommy have become volunteers. I decide to skip the picnic and go to a Barnes & Noble close to 74th and Broadway. I needed to research some recent magazines.

I go through every magazine I can think of, to no avail. Frustrated at my inability to think of a way of to locate her, I go into a bar—the same one where I met Shirley. I order my usual Corona, my favorite Mexican beer. I scan the six television screens featuring different stations, all on silent mode. To my amazement, for one instant I glimpse Natalia onscreen. She's greeting a leader of some country who has just arrived for the annual United Nations General Assembly conference. I check the channel: NBC channel seven, the same network where Marcello works.

I call Marcello. He is on the Staten Island Ferry, so cellular reception isn't good, but he understands enough to agree to meet me at Rockefeller Center.

I explain everything to him, and he goes to the station to see if he can get additional information. I have the exact hour of the transmission. I'm going to go to the UN to see if I can find out which dignitaries arrived today. I try to google the information, but I'm unable to find anything accurate.

Nevertheless, I begin to feel that challenge and the nearness that I felt when I first saw her. I'm going to find her. I know she's interested in me. If she weren't, she never would have appeared at Starbucks. I even go back to Starbucks to talk to the manager, to see if they have a video of her entering the store. I know they have, but the weekend manager doesn't know me and thinks I'm some kind of nut.

Marcello returns empty-handed. "The people I know only work during the week. I can check on Monday."

In desperation, I call Pedro's cell phone. "No worries," he says. "I know how to find out." In no time, Pedro calls back saying the UN leader is Milos Zeman, the President of the Czech Republic. He arrived at Kennedy Airport at 2 p.m. where he was greeted by a welcoming party from the UN and the Czech Embassy. He's staying at the Peninsula New York on 5th Ave and W 55th."

I relay the information to Marcello and add, "That's close. We can walk."

"Wait a minute, Mitch," he says. "They won't let you in wearing those clothes."

Pedro had mentioned that there would be a reception this evening at 8 p.m. at the hotel. We hurry back to the apartment and change, and then head to the Peninsula Hotel. We climb the short red-carpeted flight between the white stone lions and attempt to enter the hotel, but the doorman stops us. "Sorry, sir. Only guests allowed this evening. We're full of added security because we have six presidents staying here."

I decide that I have two options: Wait outside until she arrives and shout her name so she sees me, or see if I can get a room at the hotel for the night. This way security will let me inside the lobby. I call for a reservation. They have rooms— starting at $800. I desist with that idea.

Marcello accompanies me to Bloomingdale's where I purchase new clothes. I decide to buy a suit, shirt, and matching tie, as well as elegant new shoes and a belt. Before dieting, I was a size 34. Now I'm a size 36—and these suit trousers are already tight. I've gained so much weight in such a short time. I keep the receipt in my pocket, because I always lose them when they're in the bag. I know I'm going to have to return the suit and extra pants because I'm going to gain more weight. Besides, I don't need a suit. In fact, my last suit was the one my parents bought me for my bar mitzvah when I was thirteen.

I carry my packages home where I take a cold shower and relax. Marcello has made a date with a girl he met on the ferry. I want to tell him he can go after Leslie, that I'm sure, but I don't dare.

CHAPTER 46

THE PARTY

When my cell phone rings around 7 p.m., the number is unknown. I am about to dismiss the call since I get twenty unsolicited calls a day that I block immediately, but for some reason, I answer this one.

"I'm sorry I didn't come, and I'm sorry I didn't call you." It's Natalia. "I wrote down your number on a scrap of paper, and I didn't find it until five seconds ago. It was in the bottom of the purse I used yesterday."

"Oh, thank you for calling! You don't know what I've been going through trying to find you. I went back to the diner where we met twice, hoping to see you."

"You did? Can you prove that? I went to that Starbucks, but I couldn't find anyone who knows you since I only know your first name—Michael."

"My name is Mitch, not Michael, and yes, I definitely can prove that."

"Sorry." This is when I notice her Slavic accent. She must

be a Czech citizen. "Are you dressed for the reception to-night?" She is surprised at this.

"So you have really investigated me. Can you come?"

"What? Are you serious?"

"Yes. If you're with me, you don't need an invitation."

"Yes, I can come."

"Good. The Peninsula Hotel at 8 p.m. Do you want to be picked up, or can you meet me at the hotel?"

"Do you drive in Manhattan?"

"No. One of my father's drivers can pick you up."

"I'll see you there at eight."

"Please call me when you arrive, so I can have security escort you to our room."

"Bye—it was great to hear from you." She has hung up, but I don't care. A state-of-mind reversal has occurred. I've gone from total depression a few hours ago, to total exaltation now. I am a blissful man. I'm also in a state of curiosity unknown to the human mind. To my mind.

I take an Uber and called her precisely at eight. A moment later, a security guard greets me. Without asking for identification, he escorts me past the check-in barriers for reception guests. Then I see Natalia.

She is wearing the most glamorous dress I have ever seen. She is simply beautiful. Smiling, she shakes my hand and welcomes me to the President of the Czech Republic's reception. She's her uncle the President's greeter. She quickly explains that she'll join me as soon as the guests have arrived. While she's busy, I walk around the spectacular reception room, recognizing well-known governors and senators as well as ambassadors from various countries. I also observe people from non-western countries in their native dress.

The United Nations Secretary-General António Guterres has arrived. All the guests applaud. This environment is definitely not one that I'm used to, but I like it. Many of the guests know each other, and, champagne glasses in hand, they greet and toast each other. A lady dressed in green approaches me and introduces herself as the widow of the late duke of an Austrian duchy.

"My pleasure to meet you," I say. "I'm Mitch Green." Since she seems to expect me to say more, I add, "I'm the director of Body Shapers Dream Team."

"Congratulations." I realize that she assumes Body Shapers Dream Team is a Broadway play. Some people who know her join us, and diplomatic conversation ensues. I excuse myself and head straight for the food trays. I haven't had dinner.

I observe the guests and compare my clothes with theirs. Although I am decently dressed for the occasion, everyone outclasses me. My one-hundred dollar suit is distinctive among the thousand dollar Burberry and Brioni suits these men are wearing. Still, I was lucky to have done that last moment shopping. I had nothing that could have passed for diplomatic reception clothes, believe me.

Natalia is the center of attention. Everyone seems to know her. I'm waiting impatiently for her to finish with her obligatory rounds, when she appears next to me. This time she gives me a light hug. She takes my hand and leads me to her uncle.

"Uncle, this is my friend, Mitch Green." Everyone rushes over to meet me. Some inquire as to the degree of our friendship. All these people are curious as to the identity of this young gentleman with the deep blue eyes holding hands with the president's niece, the *excelentissima* Natalia Zeman.

"Are your parents here?" I ask Natalia.

"They'll arrive a little later. They had to go to another country's reception first." She accepts a glass of wine from a waiter, and we toast each other.

"Here's to us and our unexpected encounter. Cheers!" I have a feeling that she's showing me off. Whenever we advance to accept greetings from the many guests, she grabs my hand as if to re-affirm her possession of me. I thoroughly enjoy what's happening. Could this be the preamble to a future relationship?

The music starts. Natalia invites me to dance, and she's a good dancer. I guess that at this moment, I think anything Natalie does is superb. I feel the first pangs of love. She is an angel, she is my dream come true.

When her parents arrive, they're greeted with respect and admiration. Then Natalia introduces us. "Mitch, these are my parents, Mr. and Mrs. Zeman."

Her mother whispers something in what I assume is Czech. Natalia whispers back, and her mother's lips curve in an enormous smile. I take this to be a positive for me.

Without warning, her mother breaks with diplomatic etiquette and kisses and hugs me.

The night is exceptional. The evening is an affair that I will not forget.

CHAPTER 47

SPECIAL SUNDAY

Alexa is not programmed for Sunday, so I sleep late. I will repeat myself: *It was a night to remember.* I will never forget it. After all the guests left, Natalia's parents, uncle and some close friends gathered. For my sake, most of the conversation was in English, but from time to time, someone would forget and speak in a different language. All these European diplomatic families seemed to speak many languages and alternate from one to another, according to who was present.

Later, when everyone left, we got to know each other better. Natalia asked me if I dated much. I told her the truth: no. She asked about the woman she saw with me at Starbucks. I explained the group's presence and their participation in my experiment. She wanted to hear all about my experiment, my future plans, and my intentions with her. European women are fast and to the point. At least this one said she did not believe in long courtships. Under other circumstances, I would have invented an excuse to get out of there, but I was hooked.

After checking in with my group via the app, I see that my presence is requested at a 2 p.m. meeting at *The Daily Flash*. Esperanza has borrowed a professional scale that measures in pounds, and the five participants are to have their first official weigh-in.

I have brunch at the Greek diner, and the same waiter is happy to hear of my encounter with the girl of my dreams. I eat too much in an attempt to compensate for yesterday's meager meals. I am so full, that I decide to walk it off going in the direction of Lower Manhattan, towards my meeting.

The results are in:

Mitch	+ 7 pounds;
Shirley	−11 pounds;
Wallis	−13 pounds;
Leslie	+ 4 pounds;
Kim	+ 4 pounds.

Scott and Kathy are pleased and excited over these first results. Kim has all the exact data. Every aspect of the experiment precisely follows the scientific gathering specifications for data regulation procedures.

I give my group a pep talk, and everyone congratulates the four main participants. Scott advises me to take it easy on my weight gain. "I think you're overdoing it. Losing so much weight will be difficult."

Marcello videotapes everything, including everyone's comments. They all go for a five-mile walk, while I go to meet Natalia.

Natalia's parents live in one of the Trump Towers on the Upper East Side. At their apartment I find pure, exquisite luxury. I am not an art specialist, but when one views valuable art, one can see the difference, and I see it. They have a Picasso, a Monet, one Dali, and I think, I recognize a Paul Cezanne. I took art appreciation as an elective, and now I appreciate what I studied in that class.

Mr. Zeman greets me, and we speak about my experiment. I see that he is not impressed with my story, so I tell him of my future plans to create an investigative news company to serve major news networks. Next Mr. Zeman asks about my family—their education and their whereabouts.

He then tells me his life's story, how he moved to the United States and depended on family investments in the USA and Europe. He explains that Natalia works for the United Nations International Public Relations Committee where she represents her birth country. She is constantly in meetings and has to travel frequently. It is an *ad honorem* job, which means that she does not receive a salary, but it is a great honor to serve one's country. Completely volunteer—but a great honor.

Natalia's mother has prepared a succulent lunch. We start without Natalia, because there is no telling exactly when she'll return. In fact, Natalia arrives an hour later. "Sorry, I was delayed. These UN meetings start on time, but we never know when they'll finish."

She is dressed beautifully. I remember that she is also an advisor to several top international fashion companies. Apparently, she dresses in what she recommends.

We enjoy a great afternoon until it's nearing 5 p.m. Reluctantly, I tell her, "I need to go to Starbucks for the group's daily 6 p.m. meeting."

Without hesitation, she says, "I want to go with you." This time she dresses appropriately: shorts, sneakers, and an Adidas top.

The meeting is pleasant. I introduce Natalia by saying, "You remember my new friend Natalia." By now, everyone knows or suspects the reality of the situation: I am a conquered man. Natalia greets everyone.

"Please admit me to the group." she says. "I will collaborate wherever you might need me, and I'll be available whenever anyone needs me." They applaud her volunteerism and welcome her, one by one, with a hug and greeting. She has a captivating personality.

CHAPTER 48

AS THE WEEKS PROGRESS, A RESUME

W e are in Week Five. On weigh-in day, I find that I have gained over eighteen pounds. It's time to reverse the diet. Now my goal is to lose as much weight as possible without getting sick. Natalia has been a great help. She has actually gotten involved with the personal problems and food distribution, and she has helped Kathy with the exercise program since Scott is busy and can't participate every day.

Leslie has started to date one of her summer job participants. She has gained enough weight to slow down her weight gain. She has heeded my advice and created an alternative adaptation, and the architect responsible immediately offered her a permanent job upon graduation.

Kim is doing very well. He's an excellent manager and technical expert in all aspects of this experiment. On Natalia's advice, he has bought new clothes and changed his photos on his Internet connections. Now he's begun contacting some girls who had avoided him because of his extreme thinness.

Marcelo, continues to video everything. He got a second job on weekends and makes an attempt at stand-up comedy at a club on First Ave. He is meeting and dating new girls all the time. I had to ask him not to have sleepovers in the apartment because he keeps disconnecting Alexa and forgetting to plug her back in—the topic of our constant discussions.

George, too, is happy. He has started going out occasionally with Kim's Vietnamese cousin. He wants to see if he can land a permanent job in New York City. Kathy and Scott seem to be always together.

My dear Shirley is incredible; she has lost over thirty-three pounds! Initially she lost faster, but as the weeks progressed, losing has gotten tougher. She continues to progress, even though her main stimulus—me—is busy with the woman of his dreams. Still, we meet every day. I show her my affection and push her through rough times—with Natalia's help, of course. Shirley has already bought new clothes twice. Her body is starting to look great!

Wallis is doing well, although he almost quit one weekend after his girlfriend dumped him for a normal-weight guy. With Shirley and the group's support, he was able to recuperate. He's lost twenty-four pounds.

Paula and Tommy are a strange combination, but it seems that something is about to develop because most days, they keep to themselves.

Esperanza is receiving two hours of conversion classes at

the temple. Mr. Petro has informed me that a meeting among us and the people whom I've selected to be my colleagues in the new company is necessary. I am going to dedicate time to my company.

CHAPTER 49

THE COMPANY ORGANIZATION STARTS

B ayley and I have met several times. We've begun the process of selecting staff and a workplace. Our meetings are in the mornings at Starbucks. Everyone knows us by now, and they welcome our presence whether we consume or not.

Bayley has offered to invest in our initial organizational expenses. Mr. Petro has given Esperanza sufficient money so that she is able invest a portion of it in our start-up. We are in the process of finishing the legal formation of the company. I have Kim involved in the paperwork. Kim also said he would contribute to the company's initial expenses. Kim is good at everything. I'm confident that he is going to do exactly what we need. After Bayley met Marcello, he suggested that we hire him. Marcello knows many people in the artistic area of the economy, which is going to be useful.

Initially we're going to assign specific projects that need investigation and reporting. We propose paying free-lance journalists on a fee-per-project basis because we can't afford to hire permanent reporters yet.

When we start to look for a small office, we run into trouble. Office space is expensive, and contracts are for twelve-month minimums. We need office furniture and supplies. We estimate that we need at least a million dollars back-up, so that detains us for a while. Natalia confides that her family could lend us the money, but I don't want to involve them in this adventure. We have a problem.

One day when Paula and Tommy were having lunch at the now famous Greek diner, Esperanza joined them and explained the problem I was having in trying to form the company. They had no idea what I was doing privately. Paula said that she had a feeling, and that their app is 99% finished. She immediately sent a WhatsApp message:

> "Special meeting this evening. Tommy and I invite everyone to dinner at a restaurant whose name I'll send within the hour. Please dress properly. This won't be a diner."

Paula contacts me separately. "Mitch, I need to explain something of great interest to you. Can you invite this man Bayley to our dinner tonight?"

I am surprised to hear from Paula because they've been keeping a low profile, although I know they've been working daily at the newspaper office. (Esperanza keeps me informed. I never see them on my visits to Mr. Petro, probably because I check in early and they arrive after 10 a.m.) Paula has also told Esperanza that she is going to rent a small apartment near the Hudson River and that she'll be moving shortly.

Paula calls and reserves a private room for 8 p.m. at Le Cirque on East 58th Street. She then informs the group of the address, and I text Mr. Bayley. Natalia has a dinner to attend, but her curiosity makes her cancel, and she tells me that she's available to assist.

LE CIRQUE

E veryone is pleasantly surprised at the invitation, and especially to Le Cirque. This place is very expensive. Natalia tells me that she has eaten here many times with different international guests. She insinuates that it is a top restaurant and that the prices are also top. We don't understand what is going on, but it's intriguing.

Paula and Tommy arrive late, carrying a projector and their laptop. "Welcome, dear friends, because that's what you all are. We have had the luck to meet you, due to our incredible guide, Mitch, who turned us all into volunteers and has us working or dieting or overeating daily without rest. He leaves no room for us to protest or decline his orders. Thank you, Mitch Green. You are special." Everyone applauds.

I stand and thank them, and then introduce Bayley. "He was my professor at college, and now he's involved in a private venture where he'll be my associate in a brand new company, thanks to Mr. Petro who has made this possible."

Paula stood again. "I—or I should say we, because this app was developed by Tommy and me—have finally completed this incredible application that we call the Body Shapers Dream Team App. This app permits all overweight individuals to constantly view their current food habits and informs them of when to eat more and when to stop eating in order to achieve their desired weight goals. We will decide with Mitch how to introduce this app to all the major app sales companies like Apple, Microsoft, Samsung, Google, etc. This product will be sold throughout the world and will be available in all languages. This application is developed by Mitch's Body Shapers Dream Team group. Please enjoy drinks and order whatever you want. Tommy and I would like to make another incredible announcement."

Tommy gets up and makes two announcements.

Then Marcello stands and asks, "Who's paying for this restaurant?"

Mr. Petro gets up saying, "I—" but Tommy interrupts him.

"Paula and I will pay, don't worry." They all laugh and order drinks, and for a while forget the incredible effect this new app will possibly create in the lives of millions of overweight men and women throughout the world.

After we finish our entrees, Tommy stands. Usually, he's silent, but now, he speaks with the strong, confident voice of a leader. "After a terrible divorce, I came to New York looking for peace and quiet, and I stumbled upon you. I'm an industrial manager and proprietor of one of the leading auto industry brake companies. I lied to you, hoping to be accepted and to be able to live a different lifestyle than the one to which I was accustomed." He looks around at the faces, all turned to him, and his gaze rests on one of them. "Here I found people, many younger and wiser than I, one of whom is Paula. She has inspired me to create a new outlook on life. She is the most incredible and smartest person I have ever met. My divorce isn't final, but it soon will be." He takes a box from his coat pocket, and from the box, he takes a diamond ring the size of a small cherry. "Paula, will you be my wife?" She starts to cry, and her emotion is startling. Most of the group cries at this emotive moment.

"I'm so moved. I never thought I'd find a man who would be able to deal with me and be my equal." Paula wipes tears from her cheeks. "Oh, yes, Tommy. I accept. You are the greatest." She looks at all of us. "Dear friends, Esperanza let us know that Mitch has another incredible project. I investigated, and Tommy and I not only wish you success, but we want to invest $30 million dollars in your startup."

Mitch, Petro, Esperanza, Natalia, Bayley— everyone gasps. Is this really happening? This is too incredible—oh my God.

Paula continues. "I'm the CEO of one of the biggest startups in the nation, and Tommy will still be a multimillionaire after he settles with his ex-wife. So this offer is but a small amount of our personal wealth. We love all of you, and we want you all to benefit from our investment. With the permission of our natural leader and promoter Mitch, I propose that the profits from the app—and I know they will be huge—should be divided equally among this incredible dream team. I include Tommy and me, because we're part of the team. We want to share our contribution with the people who helped us find each other."

Mitch and the team are incredulous. After a long while, they calm down and analyze their new reality. Everyone congratulates Paula and Tommy, and then each other for having been able to reach these incredible goals just by volunteering for a diet experiment. Natalia and Mitch hold hands, enjoying a moment of sheer bliss.

I think everyone must have felt the same way.

CHAPTER 51

THE DIET CONTINUES

I get up very early. Alexa has been disconnected again.

Bayley and I are to meet at a lawyer's office to approve the startup's constitution and to sign all the pertinent legal paperwork. The board of directors is going to comprise the membership of the stock acquisitions group. When we sign the legal formalities, I am to have 51 % of the stock, followed by Paula and Tommy as the next main stockholders. The remaining stock is apportioned among the team. I check my WhatsApp. Everything is in order.

I've started losing weight just by going back to being my old self. I also consciously eat less, and I avoid carbs and sugars. I try to limit my food to organic. I've joined the meal group, and Scott has prepared an appropriate food schedule for me. A courier delivers the food to my office now that we have money to spend, which saves time for all of us.

Shirley is to perform a concert on Sunday, and her family plans to attend. I'm using this event as an opportunity for my parents, uncle, and siblings to meet everyone: Natalia, her family, and my group of friends. I invite them all. I tell everyone in the group to invite family and friends, and that funds will be available for those who need them. No one asks for help. We are the proud owners of an incredible app that produces real money.

CHAPTER 52

THE CONCERT AND THE END—OR IS IT THE BEGINNING?

Week nine—our final week has arrived. I am still up five pounds, but all of my old clothes already fit. I decide to donate my new clothes. Natalia goes shopping with me, and we buy clothes that she likes. I wouldn't say that I also liked—but whatever she likes, I automatically approve. Many weeks have gone by, and her magical attraction keeps increasing, never diminishing in the slightest.

Shirley is evidently nervous because this is the first time her family will see her since her weight loss. They don't even know she's been on a diet.

Shirley had difficulty sleeping last night. She couldn't control her emotions wondering how her parents would react when they saw her. She plans that they won't see her until the start of the concert. She wants to capture on video their astounded look when they first see her, so she has Kim position himself strategically to film their reaction. Shirley wants to make sure that the video will be clear because she wants this video to be historical evidence of her turn around to normalcy.

Leslie's mother has decided to come to New York. Leslie wants to introduce her to us and to her new boyfriend. She now looks more spectacular than ever, like a living doll. Mitch's advice has helped her in numerous ways. She is now independent and sure of her future goals. She knows that lack of money, her ever-present dilemma, has ended forever.

Kim has met an Irish gal through Facebook, and she's coming to meet him in person for the first time. They've seen each other on Skype and FaceTime, so their appearances won't be a surprise.

Wallis is a changed man. His girlfriend returned to him after seeing his weight loss, and they've decided to marry. They've been in love for years, but his obesity turned her off. Her family's constant bullying and criticisms regarding Wallis' weight didn't help.

Marcello didn't invite his family, but he has a new Chinese girlfriend. After the concert, he's flying to Shanghai to meet her family.

Esperanza and Mr. Petro have announced that they're pregnant. They will marry as soon as her conversion and his divorce become final. Esperanza asked if she could bring her niece Graciela and Graciela's fiancé Carlos to the concert.

Kathy's New Zealand family is to arrive on Friday. Kathy and Scott plan a fast wedding in Reno near Scott's parents' farm.

Carol is due to return this weekend. I have already prepared the apartment to make her happy. Natalia supervised, and that means perfectionism par excellence. Natalie and I know that we will marry, but right now we're absorbed with organizing our future company.

We also invite Mr. Bayley, who feels like part of the Dream Team. He doesn't have a partner, but all these last minute romantic moments have created a need in his heart. When he sees Leslie's mother, he immediately becomes fascinated with this fun-loving, beautiful, and intriguing woman. He has a sensation that had disappeared long ago—the need for a permanent companion.

The concert is a total success. Shirley is well on the road to success. When her family sees the results of her diet, they don't believe all that has happened—and in such a short time. Shirley's third cousin, who happened to come along, immediately starts dating her, so she is in seventh heaven.

CHAPTER 53

CONCLUSION

W
e meet one last time as a team. I have been able to write a great investigative report on the effects of our experiment in which we supply accurate proof for all the results.

We've been successful in our attempts to change the lives of four people: two fat ones and two skinny ones. The diets will have to continue, but without the supervision of a team. The participants have learned to apply the rules themselves.

The new app is to help all humanity. I have proven to the world that it is easy to gain weight, but hard to lose it. Still, everything is possible.

My conclusions are:

Try a diet with protein as your principal source of food.
Eat a big breakfast.
Beware of sugary foods. Don't drink more than one soda
   a week.

Eat carbohydrates but only sometimes, keeping in mind
    that they make you fat fast.
Drink a lot of liquids. Exercise as much as you can.
Don't overdo anything. Get a good night's sleep.
Don't overeat. Eat slowly.
Eat small but frequent snacks.
Love life, and keep healthy so that you can enjoy life.

                          —"Body Shapers Dream Team"

ABOUT THE AUTHOR

David Singer wears many hats: dentist, educator, communicator, lecturer, traveler, and writer. Born in Chernovitz, Romania, he speaks English and Spanish. Before coming to the USA, he lived in Argentina and the Dominican Republic. Singer received his BA degree in biology from Long Island's Hofstra University. He completed his *Odontologo* studies (equivalent to DDS) at Caracas' Central University of Venezuela School of Dentistry, and was in private practice for over forty years. At the dental school, Singer was instrumental in educating dental faculty in English terminology found in scientific journals. While in Caracas, Singer founded and edited the dental newsletter *Exito Dental*. He also taught English as a second language at the Centro Venezolano Americano; the Colegio San Ignacio de Loyola; and the Academia Americana. He founded Caracas' Rotary Club Metropolitano and has been active in several community groups. Singer is the author of *The Mind Reader* (CreateSpace, 2017). He is married to Blima Poplicher with whom he shares three children and nine grandchildren.

Made in the USA
Middletown, DE
10 May 2022

65599967R00106